MW01178228

COMMENTARIES ON
INTERNATIONAL
POLITICAL ECONOMY

To Hugh Segal
With my best wishes
            Sidney Weintraub

Significant Issues Series

Timely books presenting current CSIS research and analysis of interest to the academic, business, government, and policy communities.

Managing editor: Roberta L. Howard

For four decades, the **Center for Strategic and International Studies (CSIS)** has been dedicated to providing world leaders with strategic insights on—and policy solutions to—current and emerging global issues.

CSIS is led by John J. Hamre, formerly deputy secretary of defense, who has been president and CEO since April 2000. It is guided by a board of trustees chaired by former senator Sam Nunn and consisting of prominent individuals from both the public and private sectors.

The CSIS staff of 190 researchers and support staff focus primarily on three subject areas. First, CSIS addresses the full spectrum of new challenges to national and international security. Second, it maintains resident experts on all of the world's major geographical regions. Third, it is committed to helping to develop new methods of governance for the global age; to this end, CSIS has programs on technology and public policy, international trade and finance, and energy.

Headquartered in Washington, D.C., CSIS is private, bipartisan, and tax-exempt. CSIS does not take specific policy positions; accordingly, all views expressed herein should be understood to be solely those of the author.

The CSIS Press

Center for Strategic and International Studies
1800 K Street, N.W., Washington, D.C. 20006
Telephone: (202) 887-0200 Fax: (202) 775-3199
E-mail: books@csis.org Web: www.csis.org

COMMENTARIES ON INTERNATIONAL POLITICAL ECONOMY

CONSTRUCTIVE IRREVERENCE

SIDNEY WEINTRAUB

THE CSIS PRESS

Center for Strategic
and International Studies

Washington, D.C.

Significant Issues Series, Volume 26, Number 2
© 2004 by Center for Strategic and International Studies
Washington, D.C. 20006
All rights reserved
Printed on recycled paper in the United States of America
Cover design by Robert L. Wiser, Silver Spring, Md.
Cover photograph: © Images.com/CORBIS

08 07 06 05 04   5 4 3 2 1

ISSN 0736-7136
ISBN 0-89206-440-4

Library of Congress Cataloging-in-Publication Data

Weintraub, Sidney, 1922–
Commentaries on international political economy : constructive irreverence /
Sidney Weintraub.
     p. cm. — (Significant issues series ; v. 26, no. 2)
Collection of essays written between 2000 and 2003.
Includes bibliographical references and index.
   ISBN 0-89206-440-4
1. International economic relations. 2. Economic policy. 3. Free
trade. 4. United States—Foreign economic relations—Latin America. 5.
Latin America—Foreign economic relations—United States. I. Title. II.
Series.
HF1359.W445 2003
337—dc22
                         2003025251

CONTENTS

PREFACE

I started writing and distributing these essays, *Issues in International Political Economy*, in January 2000, and the collection in this volume contains all those that have been written since then. My motive for undertaking the series was to do what a think tank is supposed to do—namely, to describe and analyze important policy themes, express opinions, and disseminate these widely to interested audiences. The audience is worldwide. Though the emphasis is on Latin America and the Caribbean region, comments and queries come from all continents, usually from policymakers, academics, students, and business people. My purpose, simply, is to provide a service from my vantage point in Washington, D.C.

The pieces deal with political-economic policy but sometimes stray beyond that confine. For purposes of organization, I have divided the essays into five thematic categories; the choice of what pieces to include in each category is somewhat arbitrary but, I hope, logical.

The individual essays are distributed in the middle of each month, mostly via the Internet with a hyperlink to the CSIS Web site (www.csis.org). Some copies are sent by fax to those who request this. The database has become quite large, as new requests come regularly for inclusion on the distribution list, and the initial distribution for each issue now numbers about 2,000. All the essays are included on the CSIS Web site, and we can tell from the commentaries we receive that the readership is quite large, probably greater than the direct distribution.

Many recipients tell us that they forward each new essay to friends and colleagues. In addition, we get frequent requests from editors of newspapers, journals, newsletters, and the like, for permission to reprint pieces, citing CSIS as the source, and these are usually granted. Many academics seek permission to use the essays as required reading material for their students, and others use them without asking our consent. Many foreign embassies comment on specific essays, particularly if they deal with their country or geographic region. Consequently, we are convinced that the essays reach a wide audience. By selecting the initial readership, we are able to assure ourselves that we reach many important policymakers.

I choose the topics for each essay. The opinions given are mine and not those of CSIS as an institution. The comments received from readers are generally friendly, frequently agreeing with what I wrote, sometimes not, but usually expressing thanks for receiving the pieces.

I could never get these pieces out in a timely fashion without the help of my research assistants, Rebecca Tunstall at first and, after she left to pursue graduate studies, Veronica Prado. The CSIS publications office provides invaluable and timely editing help, and the CSIS webmaster has been extremely cooperative in helping me meet my mid-month dissemination deadlines.

Sidney Weintraub
William E. Simon Chair in Political Economy, CSIS
Cuernavaca, Mexico

PART ONE

TRADE AND DEVELOPMENT

After the countries of Latin America and the Caribbean (LAC) discarded import substitution, the need to grow their exports became vital to their economic development. This, in turn, required lowering import barriers, especially for the intermediate and capital goods that were inputs to their manufacturing processes.

Countries reduced their import restrictions in different ways. Chile unilaterally reduced its tariffs and adopted a uniform tariff in order not to favor some products over others; it then deliberately adopted a policy of concluding many free-trade agreements (FTAs) in the hope of diversifying its export markets. Mexico also reduced import restrictions on its own (i.e., without reciprocity), joined the General Agreement on Tariffs and Trade (GATT), and then negotiated for reciprocal concessions globally and bilaterally, also using FTAs as a deliberate technique for export expansion and market diversification.

Almost all LAC countries initially reduced import barriers unilaterally—up to a point—and then negotiated to receive reciprocal benefits for their exports; and almost all of them also entered into bilateral and plurilateral economic integration agreements. LAC now has four subregional trade agreements, in addition to the North American Free Trade Agreement (NAFTA):

- Mercosur, the common market of the South (Argentina, Brazil, Paraguay, and Uruguay);

- the Andean Group (Bolivia, Colombia, Ecuador, Peru, and Venezuela);

- the Central American Common Market (Costa Rica, El Salvador, Guatemala, Honduras, and Nicaragua); and

- Caricom, the Caribbean Community (Antigua, Barbuda, Belize, Bahamas, Barbados, Dominica, Grenada, Guyana, Haiti, Jamaica, Montserrat, St. Kitts and Nevis, Saint Lucia, St. Vincent and the Grenadines, Suriname, Trinidad and Tobago).

The LAC countries also found that their post–import substitution model had other imperatives if they were to become successful exporters. Perhaps the most important was to find the capital for investment for efficient production. This could come from internal resources, which were scarce in these low-saving countries, or from foreign investment. Foreign direct investment (FDI) during the import-substitution period was tolerated and subject to onerous conditions, and it was not plentiful except for raw materials, especially mining, and public utilities. What was needed now was FDI for manufacturing and sophisticated services, and, consequently, policies were altered to attract this. Trade and investment under the new model are inseparable, and it is hard to demarcate precise lines where one ends and the other begins.

Exports of non-primary products hardly mattered when LAC countries looked inward for their development stimuli. When challenged about ignoring exports, theorists in LAC countries developed what was essentially a self-justifying rationale that is generally referred to as "export pessimism." The argument was that it did not matter if exports to the more developed countries flourished because this very success would lead to protective restrictions to cut off these exports. Many examples of this can be cited, such as textile products, processed agricultural goods, and shoes. However, while LAC exports with higher value-added languished, those from Northeast and Southeast Asia to the industrial world flourished. And as their exports flourished, the economies of the East Asian countries grew significantly more than those of the LAC countries. One example is worth mentioning: in 1960, income per capita in South Korea was $904 and in Mexico $2,836; in 1980, just before the collapse of the import-substitution model in Mexico, the respective per capita incomes were South Korea $3,093 and Mexico $6,054. At the end of 2002, the comparative figures were Korea $9,930 and Mexico $5,910.[1]

The new model required not only complex structural changes in the LAC countries, but also the assurance of open markets in the industrial countries. For LAC, the critical market was the United States. For LAC as a whole, the United States is the destination of about 50 percent of the value of all exports. The percentages are higher for northern LAC than for countries in the Southern Cone of South America. But even in the latter, the United States is the first or second most important export destination and generally the first market for higher value-added manufactured products.

U.S. economists, and even the U.S. government, long preached the futility of import substitution as a long-term development strategy. When the change came, however, the United States did not always practice what its preachings implied. Imports of manufactured and agricultural products from low-wage LAC countries remained subject to severe import restrictions in the United States. The approval of NAFTA required an arduous effort precisely because there was deep concern in the United States about competing with low-wage imports. This concern remains to this day and has made liberal U.S. trade policy a highly conflictive proposition.

GROWING TRADE: NECESSARY BUT NOT SUFFICIENT

Higher and growing levels of exports are by no means a complete path to higher growth rates. It is an important element of growth, as Japan and South Korea amply demonstrated in their time, but other policies must operate in conjunction with export expansion. Mexico has learned this lesson. Exports from Mexico have grown at an annual rate of 13 percent since NAFTA came into existence, but growth in gross domestic product over this same period has been a modest 3 percent a year. The reasons for this are largely inadequate macroeconomic and structural policies. Mexico had an economic crisis at the end of 1994, the year NAFTA came into existence, largely because of excessive fiscal expenditures (via development banks, which were off-budget) and an overvalued peso that collapsed. Mexico today has prudent fiscal and monetary policies but low tax collection and an energy policy that puts increasingly severe limits on industrial expansion. Brazil was long limited in its ability to practice sound fiscal policy because of the burden of expenditures for pensions.

The Doha Round of trade negotiations in progress in the World Trade Organization was named the "development round" in recognition that the issue is not trade per se, but rather one of increased trade in the interest of development. The development aspects deal primarily with the reduction of industrial country barriers on products in which developing countries are competitive, especially agricultural products, which are heavily subsidized in the developed countries—that is, in the European Union, Japan, and the United States.

CURRENT TRADE STRUCTURE

The import-substitution development model foundered essentially because economic growth was centered on development from within individual countries, and few countries in LAC were large enough to sustain this even briefly. Brazil and Mexico were large enough economically for import substitution to provide a launching pad for growth, but with a limited time horizon. In recognition of this reality, the LAC countries entered into economic integration agreements designed to enlarge markets while retaining import substitution. The Latin American Free Trade Association (LAFTA) was created for this reason. The countries that benefited most from LAFTA were those that had the most advanced industrial structures, mainly Brazil and Mexico. The LAC countries also discovered that even all of LAC was not large enough economically to sustain growth via inward-looking development policy.

The new-style integration agreements in LAC are referred to as "open" integration in contrast to the older, closed model. They are based, at least in principle, on relatively low import barriers against nonmember countries and an outward-looking rather than an inward-looking orientation. NAFTA, for Mexico, was a profound policy shift—one not only looking outward toward the United States and Canada, but also seeking trade access to and investment from the world's largest economic power. With NAFTA, the two countries ceased to be such "distant neighbors," as Alan Riding had described them. Mexico, as noted above, has also signed many FTAs, both in the Western Hemisphere and elsewhere, especially with the European Union.

Just about all LAC countries have engaged in what legitimately can be called an orgy of bilateral and plurilateral FTAs, mostly within the hemisphere, but some with outside countries. It is hard to count the precise number, because some agreements overlap, but the total now exceeds 30. The United States, which embarked in a substantial way on bilateral FTAs when it reached an agreement with Canada that went into effect in 1989, has since expanded this practice. In the hemisphere, the United States now has FTAs in NAFTA (with Canada and Mexico) and with Chile, and is negotiating for an FTA with the five countries of the Central American Common Market. In addition, the United States has FTAs with Israel, Jordan, and Singapore, and is contemplating further FTAs with Morocco and Bahrain. The European Union has its own large array of FTAs. Japan, which until recently did not have any FTAs, has now embarked on this practice.

The world is now saturated with FTAs and other preferential economic agreements, to the extent that as much trade is conducted preferentially as under the core principle of the GATT and the WTO, that of most-favored-nation (MFN)—that is, under conditions of nondiscrimination. The patterns of cross-discrimination are almost impossible to decipher because they affect overlapping pairs of countries. The rules of origin in the various FTAs (these are needed to determine what products are granted free entry under the agreements) differ, as do the dispute-settlement arrangements. Producers operating in several countries often choose the precise location for production and export shipment based on the discrimination or preferences that exist. For example, before the United States concluded an FTA with Chile, many U.S. companies chose Canada as the production site to avoid Chile's MFN tariff because Canada had an FTA with Chile. In other words, location rather than efficiency determined where much production took place. This is now taking place throughout the hemisphere.

There is also a cost in political relations when an FTA is concluded with one country and not another. This cost can be high for the United States because equal access to its large market is crucial for many countries. U.S. policymakers no doubt believe that this discrimination sets up incentives for non-preferred countries to seek FTAs with the United States and to adjust their policies accordingly, but this can be a time-consuming process.

Each bilateral FTA is a modern form of mercantilism—a desire to preferentially increase trade. It is, as well, a form of beggar-thy-neighbor policy because of its discriminatory aspects. The world has come a long way from the postwar ideal of equal treatment (MFN) for all across the globe.

The attraction of a comprehensive Free Trade Area of the Americas (FTAA) is that it has the potential to remove the differential treatment among hemispheric countries and simultaneously establish a single set of rules of origin and dispute-settlement procedures. Businesses that export into many countries surely would welcome this simplification. It is most unlikely, however, that the FTAA will be this comprehensive. Many countries have taken or wish to take key issues off the negotiating table. The United States has removed the negotiation of agricultural subsidies and antidumping duties from FTAA negotiations, reserving these for global negotiations in the WTO; the Brazilians wish to remove intellectual property; other LAC countries wish to remove trade in a number of services or opening government procurement to international competition or establishing clear rules for investment. It is hard to predict the scope of the FTAA at this stage of the negotiations, but the final agreement—assuming there is one—is unlikely to be as thorough as originally contemplated.

The WTO is the main negotiating forum. It is already severely damaged from the failure of the Cancún meeting of trade ministers in September 2003, and weakening it further would have seriously adverse consequences on the world trading system. Reducing or, better still, eliminating subsidies to producers and exporters of many agricultural products in the developed countries is a central issue if the Doha round is to be a development round. The lower the MFN duties are globally, the less scope there is for meaningful tariff preferences. A successful Doha Round is the key to reversing some of the spaghetti bowl of bilateral preferential agreements that have sprung up over the last 10 to 15 years.

We are at a pivotal moment for global trade policy. An overload of trade negotiations is taking place at once—more preferential bilateral and plurilateral negotiations, a regional negotiation designed to include all of the Western Hemisphere, and what is intended to be a comprehensive round of global trade bargains in the WTO. The priorities should be the WTO first, the FTAA second, and only then the bilateral FTAs being negotiated throughout the world. It is by no means clear, however, that these are the priorities of the main players in the game of global trade.

Note

[1] These data come from *World Development Indicators 2003* (Washington, D.C.: World Bank, 2003).

1   TRADE POLICY AFTER SEATTLE*

The failure of the WTO ministerial talks [November 30–December 3, 1999] was either a wake-up call to governments that the post-World War II objective of moving ever closer to free trade is no longer acceptable, a playground for professional protesters and anarchists, or some combination of the two. Commentary on what went wrong at Seattle is voluminous and the purpose here is not to add to this verbiage. The intent, rather, is to look ahead.

One major difference between what happened after the two world wars in the twentieth century was the protectionist disaster after the first, and the progressive opening to trade that was the hallmark of the world community after the second. One lesson of this contrasting history is that protectionist passion has an unacceptably high price tag while open markets contribute to prosperity—certainly in the United States.

Yet the reality is that the WTO ministers in Seattle were unable to move ahead, due partly to the demonstrators and partly to irreconcilable positions of key countries. The United States contributed to this by offering little and demanding much and insisting that violations of core labor principles should result in trade sanctions against developing countries. The major industrial countries—the United States, the European Union, and Japan—were more concerned with domestic politics than world comity.

The following are some suggestions for reviving the trade discussions:

- The dispute-settlement mechanism should be opened to "friend of the court" submissions before the panelists present their final opinions. Some sunshine would remove one element of justifiable complaint against the WTO.

- Bring the International Labor Organization (ILO) more into the negotiating process as the protector of core labor principles. This would not completely satisfy any of the contending parties, but would bring the most expert organization on core labor rights into the trade picture in a constructive way.

---

* *Issues in International Political Economy*, no. 1 (January 2000).

- The most vitriolic trade disputes in the environmental field have arisen from the U.S. tendency to make the rules unilaterally (as in the tuna-dolphin and turtle-shrimp cases) and then to protest vehemently when WTO (or GATT) panels argued these were discriminatory. What is needed is some way to reconcile mutual good intentions, those of environmentalists in rich and poor countries alike, with a more inclusive decisionmaking process.

- There is a "built-in" agenda left over from the Uruguay Round to deal with agriculture and services. Such negotiations will not prosper unless the key countries do not rule solutions to be off the table at the outset, as was largely the case for agriculture at Seattle.

- This admonition must prevail as well on antidumping duties, where the United States argued that it had no give in its position. This is becoming a losing effort as time passes because other countries are increasingly emulating the United States in applying antidumping duties.

- There are sectors in which trade can be liberalized without tradeoffs in other sectors. Finance and telecommunications are examples. These "zero-for-zero" negotiations should move ahead wherever feasible.

- Decisionmaking in the WTO must be improved. The GATT worked on the basis of consensus, which really meant that the powerful nations dictated the agenda. This is not a practical formula for an organization that may soon have 150 members. The breakdown of the consensus model was apparent when the WTO members recently could not agree on choosing either a New Zealander or a Thai for a six-year term as director general and were forced to settle on three-year terms for each. What the WTO needs is a smaller executive committee with, perhaps, 20 to 25 members from both developed and developing countries to hammer out compromises before submitting these for consensus approval.

Two other background realities must be factored in to any trade analysis. The first is that much of the antipathy toward the WTO reflects deep-rooted concern in developed and developing countries alike about the effects of globalization—the vast international movement of capital, the spread of production throughout the world, the ability to move goods and services rapidly, the increase of trade in component parts rather than finished products. It is evident that this means some loss of domestic control over events and is a natural target for nationalistic demagoguery. The fact that globalization is largely led by multinational corporations able to take advantage of transportation and communication advances heightens the fear of loss of national control.

The second is that previous rounds of GATT trade negotiations have been made possible by U.S. leadership and this has not been present during the past few years. The pathbreaking effort to reach a Free Trade Area of the Americas is being stalled by the lack of fast-track authority for the U.S. president, and there is little prospect that this will change until the next administration, if even then. Another WTO round will similarly require fast-track authority. Without this—without some assurance that complex cross-sectoral deals will not be negated by a host of exceptions introduced by individual congresspersons—other countries will not be convinced of U.S. sincerity.

Globalization is a consequence of technology and will not be halted, short of a global catastrophe. The United States will not find willing partners to negotiate comprehensive trade agreements unless the U.S. body politic gives some assurance that a deal once made will not be altered in the ratification process.

The Seattle fiasco was a red alert that the process of continued global trade opening is in danger. A response to this danger requires leadership from the United States because there is nobody else. The United States is sometimes accused of triumphalism because of its awesome economic power, but recent U.S. behavior in the trade field is more wimpish than arrogant.

2   THE LABOR-TRADE LINK[*]

The effort to bring labor issues into the domain of trade negotiations has a long history. Initially, in the period after World War II, U.S. labor unions recognized that wages were necessarily lower in developing countries than in the United States, and the thrust of the effort was to impede imports from producers whose wages were lower than average in the exporting country. The effects of these efforts were negligible.

The nature of the effort changed after NAFTA was negotiated. Once again, economic logic made it hard to insist that wages in Mexico must be raised across-the-board, and the target instead emphasized satisfactory working conditions and core labor rights. These core rights are freedom of association and collective bargaining, elimination of exploitative child labor, prohibition of forced labor, and nondiscrimination in employment. These are embodied in conventions agreed to in the International Labor Organization (ILO), which, for the most part, the United States has not ratified.

The reason for linking labor issues and trade negotiations, as articulated by those who favor this, is that this provides leverage—the ability to punish when agreed standards are breached. It is unclear who would make punishment decisions, whether the importing country, as is done for antidumping duties, or a panel of experts, as is the practice for resolving other disputes in the World Trade Organization (WTO). The ILO as now constituted offers the ability to publicize violations of core labor standards but not to impose import restrictions.

The foregoing simple description of the position of U.S. labor unions makes it evident why it has attracted no support in developing countries. The motive is to punish, to turn back exports from developing countries under guidelines that will be nearly impossible to devise. Developing countries believe they are now disadvantaged in the WTO by the long-standing industrial country restrictions on textile and apparel imports, the use by rich countries of export and producer subsidies in agriculture, and the highly restrictive operation of U.S. antidumping procedures. One concern is that labor sanctions will work more or less like antidumping sanctions now work and that the mere lodging of a

---

[*] *Issues in International Political Economy*, no. 7 (July 2000).

complaint will almost always lead to a restriction against imports. The targets in the labor area will be developing countries.

Despite these misgivings by developing countries, the United States reportedly came close in Seattle to establishing a working group on trade and labor. The effort collapsed when President Clinton told a Seattle newspaper that he expected the end result of the working group to be a system of trade sanctions against countries violating the agreed standards. This was implicit from the outset (else why use the WTO), but there was no escape from the reality that this was official U.S. thinking when President Clinton made it explicit. It will be difficult, probably impossible, to recover from this setback to the U.S. stance.

The rationale put forward by U.S. labor unions, their supporters in Congress, and the administration is not that they seek import restrictions, but rather that freer trade requires more protection for workers in developing countries. Some U.S. supporters of the trade-labor linkage may believe this. But the argument has no credibility in developing countries. The prevalent view in these countries is that the United States seeks to protect labor—as long as it is American.

Two verifications of this point can be cited. President Ernesto Zedillo of Mexico, in a speech before the World Economic Forum in Davos on January 28, 2000, stated that proponents of global, homogeneous labor standards imposed as a precondition for additional trade liberalization "overlook the fact that for most people in developing countries who work in trade-related activities, their jobs mean a significant improvement with respect to their previous occupations." The *Wall Street Journal,* in a front-page article on February 28 of this year, reported on a U.S. offer to Cambodia to increase its quota for apparel exports to the United States in exchange for Cambodian actions to improve domestic wages and working conditions. If the article is correct, the Cambodians lived up to their part of the bargain, but the United States did not.

Most of the preceding argumentation is irrelevant in the current trade policy context in the United States. The labor unions and their supporters assert that low wages and unsatisfactory working conditions in developing countries disadvantage competing U.S. workers. The evidence that low labor standards give countries a competitive export advantage is questionable, according to a study by the Organization for Economic Cooperation and Development (OECD). The U.S. export community has been unwilling to accept legislation that imposes trade penalties on countries for violations of whatever labor standards are adopted by the United States. It is now apparent that such standards will not be accepted internationally in the WTO. The two sides now talk past each other. Yet, this un-joined debate is preventing passage of fast-track legislation that would permit the United States to be a full participant in either the negotiations for a Free Trade Area of the Americas or a new multilateral round in the WTO. Whatever the intent, protectionism prevails.

For those who believe that the free flow of goods and services among nations benefits both global and national welfare, the task is to figure out techniques that will let trade flourish while not prejudicing the majority of workers in developed and developing countries. The two main political parties have made no progress on this task, and the two minor party candidates, Pat Buchanan and Ralph Nader, despite their vastly different ideologies on social issues, both take positions that would result in reducing imports from developing countries.

One technique worth exploring is a mechanism under which complaints about violations of labor standards would be examined not by the WTO, but by panelists from the countries involved in the dispute, with a neutral expert as chairperson. Complaints would be limited to violations of core labor standards. If a violation were found, a monetary fine would be levied against the violating company. For reasons of sovereignty, it may be necessary to fine the offending country, with the understanding that this would be passed on to the company. The fine would go into the treasury of the country where the violation was committed for use in future domestic monitoring of labor conditions.

This suggestion is made in order to avoid trade sanctions because it is now clear that these will not be accepted by developing countries. Using the fines at home to improve working conditions has the merit of not punishing a country for the actions of some of its corporations. The right to bring a complaint should not be exclusively industrial country against developing country, but any combination in any direction. The procedure could be supervised by the ILO, thereby removing two impediments: tying labor sanctions to trade negotiations; and giving some bite to the ILO in its monitoring of labor standard violations.

Will this technique work? I don't know. It will not work if the objective of supporters of the trade-labor link is to prevent further trade liberalization. What we do know is that nothing else has worked so far to eliminate an arid debate on linking trade and labor issues—with the result that progress in further freeing of trade has been stymied.

3   NAFTA EVALUATION*

There has been an extraordinary expansion of commerce in North America since the North American Free Trade Agreement went into effect on January 1, 1994. For each of the three NAFTA countries, the percentage increase in exports to the other two has been larger than the export increase to the rest of the world from 1994 to 1999. This is shown in figure 1.

Figure 1. Average Annual Increase in Intra-NAFTA Exports vs. NAFTA Exports to Rest of World, 1994–1999

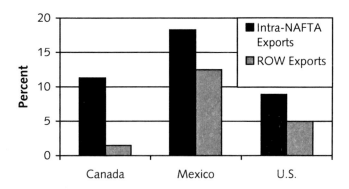

For Canada and Mexico, intra-NAFTA exports now represent between 85 and 90 percent of total exports. The U.S. proportion of intra-NAFTA exports is lower, but still amounts to 36 percent of all U.S. exports.

The non-trade aspects of NAFTA are, perhaps, more interesting because they are more enduring than annual trade figures. I will approach these non-trade issues under four headings.

INSTITUTIONAL DEVELOPMENT

Much anti-NAFTA sentiment focuses on the support of the agreement by large, multinational corporations. This is at the heart of Ralph

---

* *Issues in International Political Economy*, no. 8 (August 2000).

Nader's opposition. Most economists and academics who concentrate on North American issues are by no means in thrall to multinational corporations, yet they too support NAFTA in overwhelming numbers. Their interest is to establish a cooperative, interactive, and durable framework in North America for the benefit of all three countries. They generally have only passing interest in transitory matters that arise this month, or even this year, and then disappear. Instead, much of their focus is on institutions for deepening the interplay between nationals of the three countries in North America. This is taking place. With more than half a billion dollars of merchandise crossing the U.S-Mexico border each day, and more than a billion crossing the U.S.-Canada border each day, there is now a vast network of business relationships. Mexico has a growing and increasingly assertive environmental movement, which hardly existed earlier and probably would not exist at all if not for NAFTA. Universities throughout the three countries have inaugurated North American research and study centers. Civic organizations with cross-border connections, focusing on issues of women's and labor rights to the promotion of democracy, have mushroomed.

Institution building is not a subject of great interest to the daily media. It is hardly mentioned by critics of NAFTA. But it is the basis for constructive long-term relationships in North America, and NAFTA has played an indispensable role in institution building.

U.S. JOB LOSS AND CREATION

There are no solid data on job losses (or job gains, for that matter) from NAFTA, only anecdotal cases of companies that have closed due to import competition from, or movement of production to, Mexico. The main methodology used by those estimating U.S. job loss has been to look at the size of the U.S. trade deficit with Mexico ($23 billion last year) and then to extrapolate job loss based on some static relationship between trade deficits (surpluses) and job loss (gains). The latest figure I came across from the Economic Policy Institute was a 200,000-job loss from NAFTA.

The methodology is badly flawed. The great engine of job creation in the United States is the booming U.S. economy. Jobs are constantly lost, and jobs are created. U.S. job turnover each year is estimated by the Department of Labor at eight million. Despite an overall U.S. trade deficit that is running at an annual rate of more than $400 billion this year, the U.S. unemployment rate hovers around 4 percent (i.e., the U.S. economy is operating at full employment).

The number of U.S. jobs created since 1994, when NAFTA began, has been around 15 million. By contrast, the number of workers actually taking up the support that has been approved for retraining or relocating under trade adjustment assistance programs related to imports from Canada and Mexico is around 100,000 over the full six and one-half years of NAFTA. The current U.S. problem is worker shortages, not job shortages.

POLITICS OF FREE TRADE

The politics of free trade has been divisive in the United States, mainly because people do lose jobs from imports even if the economy as a whole takes this in stride. Many of the job losses, moreover, have been in mature industries that face serious import competition, such as wearing apparel. The inability of the Clinton administration to secure fast-track authority for global or hemispheric trade negotiations can be attributed to the fear of competition from imports from low-wage, developing countries.

However, there is another way to look at the politics of free trade. Mexico abandoned its long-standing import protection policy during the 1980s and then entered into free trade with the United States in 1994. Mexico, in essence, shifted from a managed, state-controlled development model to a drive for export expansion, building on low import protection. Just last month, on July 2, Mexico also achieved a democratic breakthrough when the long-entrenched Partido Revolucionario Institucional lost the presidency. Is there a connection between the adoption of an open market economy and Mexico's democratic accomplishment? I think so and will develop this theme further in the next issue of this monthly commentary. Mexico's president-elect, Vicente Fox, has made clear that his objective is to deepen NAFTA even further.

CONCERN OVER SOVEREIGNTY

The central issue in the 1988 Canadian national election was whether the free trade agreement (FTA) signed with the United States by the then-Conservative government would lead to a loss of Canadian sovereignty. The argument of the head of the Liberal Party was that one thing leads to another: first a drastic diminution of economic independence and then a loss of political sovereignty. The Conservatives won the 1988 election, and the FTA went into effect on January 1, 1989. When the Liberals returned to power, their previous position was jettisoned, and the FTA was supported. The Liberals went further: they joined NAFTA, have since signed a FTA with Chile, and are strong supporters of the Free Trade Area of the Americas. The issue of loss of Canadian sovereignty stemming from free trade is now a dead letter, except at the margins of Canadian society. English Canada has concerns about protecting its cultural identity, but the old fear about free trade destroying the national ability to determine the important aspects of economic and political life is gone.

Few influential Mexicans show any concern over a loss of sovereignty stemming from free trade. These old positions, once so important in our two neighboring countries, have been transferred to the United States, to the most powerful of the three NAFTA members. When the argument is made that free trade deprives the United States of economic sovereignty, as it frequently is, it is usually a subterfuge for protectionism. As Americans, it is far better to have prosperous rather than struggling neighbors, and NAFTA contributes to this objective.

4 TELLING IT LIKE IT IS[*]

This is my curmudgeon commentary. Its barbs are directed against exaggeration, double-talk, and scapegoating of important institutions engaged in global economic development.

I do not intend, in what follows, to disparage the importance of labor unions in protecting the rights and benefits of workers, or to argue that the United States is a protectionist nation, or to doubt the valuable work that is done by multilateral institutions. My purpose, rather, is to highlight a few points: the hypocrisy that exists when imports of goods and services from poor countries are restricted while simultaneously insisting that this exclusion will benefit workers in those countries; the inconsistency of promoting democracy in developing countries even as we neglect the interplay of foreign trade, economic well-being, and political outcomes; the perpetuation of the fiction that multilateral institutions are independent actors that behave supranationally in ways that conflict with the desires of their powerful members; and the misconception that institutions such as the World Bank provide a service by promising more than they can deliver.

The leaders of organized labor in the United States opposed NAFTA and the grant of permanent normal trading relations with China. They are also against a free trade area of the Americas and opening a new round of negotiations in the World Trade Organization. The stated basis for this opposition is that the United States should not further liberalize its import structure until other countries accept core labor standards (right of association, power to organize and bargain collectively, prohibition against forced labor, minimum age for employment of children, and acceptable working conditions), and that punishment should be meted out in the form of U.S. import restrictions when these standards are violated.

Is this protectionism or a socially conscious initiative to upgrade labor conditions in poor countries? The leaders of poor countries insist that they, too, want to raise labor standards, but cannot do this if their export earnings are restricted. The practical result of the U.S. position is that meaningful trade negotiations are not going forward. Even

---

[*] *Issues in International Political Economy*, no. 10 (October 2000).

though labor leaders insist this is not about protectionism, it sure looks like protectionism. (Former senator Dale Bumpers has noted that when politicians say something is not about money, it is about money.)

World Bank analysis has shown persuasively that the developing countries that have made the most progress in raising incomes are those that have opened their markets and engaged actively in world trade. However, there are still anti-trade advocates who advise today's developing countries to look inward, just as many of today's developed countries focused first on internal markets and protecting their producers against foreign competitors. This was Alexander Hamilton's advice to the newborn United States. It was the development pattern for Japan. It was Raúl Prebisch's advice to Latin American countries. Although this advice may have had some relevance once upon a time for countries with large or potentially large internal markets, such as Brazil, it surely does not for countries with tiny markets, like many in Latin America, the Caribbean, and Africa. The lesson of post–World War II development history is that countries that looked outward, such as those in East Asia, grew rapidly, while those that looked inward, as in Latin America, were relatively stagnant.

Is the advice to poor countries to look inward in the modern and increasingly globalizing world sincere, or is it designed to prevent competition in the U.S. market? Why advise developing countries to emulate the world's losers rather than the winners?

A dominant aspect of U.S. foreign policy today is to promote democracy wherever this seems feasible, such as in Latin America and the Caribbean, East Asia, Africa, and the transition nations of the former Soviet Union. This is a laudable effort. At the same time, however, the most severe U.S. trade restrictions are directed against imports from developing countries—such as sugar and textile products from just about everywhere, orange juice from Brazil, and steel from many developed and developing countries alike. U.S. foreign aid now represents 0.1 percent of our gross national product, placing the United States at the bottom of the list of donor countries. Our slogan used to be "trade, not aid." Now it is more like "not too much trade and very little aid."

It is extremely difficult for poor countries to establish stable democracies. Achieving this objective is made even more complex by the inherent contradiction in U.S. policy—preaching democracy even as we limit the ability of these countries to obtain the resources necessary to make democracy possible.

During the past year much invective has been hurled at key multilateral institutions established at the end of World War II. This was evident in Seattle late last year when protesters tried to disrupt the meetings of the World Trade Organization (the successor to the General Agreement on Tariffs and Trade, which came into being in 1947), and again last month in Prague during the annual meetings of the World Bank and the International Monetary Fund. It is not clear why the demonstrations were directed against these institutions rather than at the countries that determine the institutions' policies. They are not supranational bodies, but rather creatures of their masters, the world's most powerful national governments.

It is troubling when nongovernmental organizations exercise their right of free speech by preventing delegates to international meetings from exercising their right of free speech. We should not be troubled, however, when serious nongovernmental observers act constructively to change practices they find offensive. The IMF has long been ultra-secretive about its analyses and findings; this is inappropriate for an institution that obtains its funds from national governments (i.e., from taxpayers). The WTO's dispute-settlement procedures, which are an important part of that organization's work, have themselves been overly secretive. Many of these practices are changing, and the outside critics deserve much of the credit for this greater openness.

The president of the World Bank, James Wolfensohn, has exerted great effort to make the bank's work more transparent. At the same time, he exaggerates, incorrigibly so. He implies that the bank, under his leadership, has "discovered" that economic growth, while necessary, is not sufficient to achieve widespread social development. There are many examples of this attitude. Only one will be cited: "The old approach of an exclusive focus on growth as the elixir for all the world's problems is thus too circumscribed."[1] Wolfensohn's emphasis on alleviating poverty is praiseworthy, but the trashing of all the foreign aid practitioners who preceded him for not understanding the multiple aspects of development is egregiously inaccurate and ungracious.

The World Bank's *World Development Report 2000/2001* is devoted exclusively to "attacking poverty." It approaches this theme citing three areas for action: creating opportunities, empowering the poor, and providing greater security against the risks the poor face. The study contains a mountain of data and undoubtedly will be a valuable reference source for years to come. What it fails to do, however, is to explain

how the World Bank can achieve these goals, particularly empower-
ment, which it admits depends on "the interaction of political, social,
and other institutional processes." Is this the role of the World Bank?

Note

[1] James Wolfensohn and Joseph Stiglitz, *Financial Times*, September 22, 1999.

5   BEHIND THE TRADE ISSUES FACING PRESIDENT BUSH[*]

The shorthand explanation for the lack of bipartisan consensus in the United States for moving ahead on a new, comprehensive trade initiative is that there is disagreement about how to link labor and environmental issues with trade negotiations.

Stated simply, the accepted analysis runs along the following lines. The mainstream of the Democratic Party in the U.S. Congress wants these linkages in the body of any new, comprehensive agreement (that is, not in a side agreement and not necessarily in a single-issue agreement, such as on financial services or telecommunications), with provision for trade sanctions in the event any partner country violates the agreed standards. The issue is most intense with respect to core labor issues because organized labor, which heavily backed the Democrats in the recent elections, speaks with one voice. The leading environmental organizations differ as to how they can best accomplish their objective of assuring that increased trade and investment do not result in environmental degradation; the environmental movement, unlike organized labor, is not anti-import in its approach. The mainstream of the Republican Party in the Congress, reflecting the sentiment of large multinational corporations heavily involved in international trade, is fearful that authorization for a new type of trade penalty will lead inexorably to a plethora of import restrictions.

The foregoing analysis is generally correct, but it omits too much. It leaves too many motives unstated and fails to capture the priorities of the various contenders.

Organized labor is most powerful in the United States in industries that must compete head-to-head with imports—such as textiles and apparel, steel, and autos. Union leaders surely care about working conditions and labor rights in developing countries, but they are equally concerned with competing imports and investment moving abroad into import-sensitive sectors. The latter concern was evident in the long bickering over African and Caribbean Basin preferences for apparel, the support for renewal of Japan's voluntary restraints on auto exports,

---

[*] *Issues in International Political Economy*, no. 13 (January 2001).

the cacophony of complaints about automotive imports from Mexico, and the durable efforts of steel workers to force limits on steel imports.

Organized labor is content with stalemate on comprehensive trade negotiations and, by extension, with stalemate on a labor-trade linkage that might lead to serious trade negotiations.

Business interests in the United States went all out to secure congressional approval of permanent normal trading relations with China, but did not make a comparable effort to help President Clinton secure fast-track authority from the Congress for either a new negotiating round in the World Trade Organization or to complete the bargaining for a Free Trade Area of the Americas. Equal access—equal to that enjoyed by major trade competitors—was considered crucial for the potentially immense China market, but progress in the WTO or the Western Hemisphere negotiations had much lower priority for U.S. business. A WTO negotiation would inevitably put U.S. antidumping procedures on the trading block, and this is anathema—as was evident in the lead-up to the contentious 1999 Seattle ministerial meeting. The only discrimination U.S. exports face in this hemisphere is from other hemispheric countries, and that is not overwhelming. The issue of equal access in the hemisphere would arise seriously if the European Union were to conclude a free-trade agreement with Mercosur; and, if that occurred, we can rest assured that there would be a business push for fast-track authority for the FTAA.

The Clinton administration, in its closing days, decided to negotiate bilateral free-trade agreements with Jordan (actually completed, although enabling legislation is still needed), Singapore, and Chile. The logic for this tactic was twofold: to show progress in concluding free-trade agreements; and to demonstrate that FTAs with labor and environmental conditions can be reached (although Chile prefers that these issues be in side agreements and opposes a system of trade sanctions for noncompliance). The Republican leadership in the Congress sent a letter reminding the administration of its opposition to the labor and environmental features. The danger of the Clinton administration approach—that fast-track authority is not needed in bilateral trade negotiations—is that many in the Congress will accept this reasoning and deny fast-track authority for comprehensive trade negotiations as well, and thereby stymie progress in both the WTO and the Americas.

The auguries for a successful trade initiative in the Bush administration are not good, despite the free-trade proclivity of the new president. In November 2000, the U.S. Trade Deficit Review Commission created by the Congress in October 1998 issued its final report. It is a mosaic of chapters agreed to by the six Democratic appointees and six Republican appointees and chapters on which there was no agreement. The two sides agreed on three chapters (although not without supplementary comments) and disagreed on four.

More to the point, the two sides presented thoroughly distinct visions for U.S. international economic policy. The Republicans, in essence, embraced globalization and the positive contribution this makes to the U.S. economy, whereas the Democrats asserted that globalization leads to a race to the bottom in labor rights and environmental standards. The Republicans see the trade and current account deficits as part of a "virtuous" process under which investment in the United States exceeds national savings, thereby leading to increased productive capacity. The Democrats, in contrast, see the trade deficit as originating in predatory mercantilist policies of other trading nations. Because of the date of its release, in the middle of the maneuvering of the contested presidential election, the report attracted hardly any attention. Perhaps this was fortuitous.

Patching together an agreed U.S. trade policy is not simply a task of devising anodyne words to bridge differences on dealing with labor and the environment in the context of trade negotiations. The labor-environment disagreement is a symptom, not the cause, of stalemate. The underlying issue is disagreement over how to most usefully engage the rest of the world economically—whether to further reduce barriers to trade and capital movement or to avoid these reductions on the premise that an open world trading system, replete with massive capital flows, is prejudicial to the United States.

President Bush will have to confront this issue at the Summit of the Americas in Quebec on April 20–22, 2001, that is, in the first 100 days of his administration. The main issue of the summit is to make progress toward concluding an FTAA negotiation by the agreed date of 2005, or earlier. Robert Zoellick, President Bush's designee as U.S. trade representative, is informed on both trade and Latin American matters and is, therefore, well positioned to play an important role in the summit preparations.

U.S trade policy must reconcile a seemingly incompatible dilemma between the suspicion of many leaders of developing countries that labor and environmental conditions are a subterfuge for imposing new U.S. trade restrictions, and the difficulty of obtaining congressional consent for negotiating a comprehensive agreement without these pro-visions. The new president, when he is in Quebec, may be able to test whether other important hemispheric nations, especially Brazil, will be prepared to exchange trade and related concessions in the absence of fast-track authority, that is, whether they are willing to play out their final negotiating hand without some assurance that the U.S. Congress will not upset the balance of bargains reached.

6   TRADE POLICY SUGGESTIONS FOR THE QUEBEC SUMMIT*

President Bush has just two months before he attends the third Summit of the Americas in Quebec on April 20–22. The main objective at the summit will be to make progress on reaching agreement on a Free Trade Area of the Americas by 2005 or earlier. What follows are policy matters that President Bush might address to further this objective.

APPROACH TO THE FAST-TRACK APPROVAL PROBLEM

The term should be changed to make clear that "fast-track" does not refer to speed, but rather to the fact that the United States will not re-open the details of the multilateral FTAA agreement after a reciprocal balance of concessions is reached. The new U.S. trade representative, Robert Zoellick, has suggested "trade-promotion authority," or TPA.

Why fast track is necessary:

- the unwillingness of other countries to play their full hands in a first negotiation if this can be altered subsequently by the U.S. Congress; and
- the fact that the FTAA is not like a single sector negotiation, or like the China agreement in which the United States made no concessions other than to grant permanent normal trading relations.

Two negotiations are needed:

- the first must satisfy a variety of domestic U.S. interests; and
- the second is needed to avoid imposing conditions on U.S. negotiators that would be unacceptable to their negotiating partners.

PROBLEMS THAT MUST BE ADDRESSED

Domestic audiences

Organized labor wants labor provisions in the text of the basic agreement and not in side agreements and seeks penalties for violations of core labor standards.

---

* *Issues in International Political Economy*, no. 14 (February 2001).

Environmental organizations wish to have environmental safeguards in the body of the FTAA agreement. Unlike organized labor, environmentalists are not anti-import; but no uniformity of positions exists among major environmental NGOs.

The business community has a deep concern that trade sanctions relating to labor and the environment will result in a spate of U.S. import restrictions and potential retaliations or, at best, that such provisions will lead to protracted arbitration and litigation that will defeat the purposes of trade opening.

Negotiating partners

Other countries in the hemisphere have made clear that they see labor provisions involving trade sanctions as a U.S. technique to curtail their exports. The most vociferous objections come from Brazil, by far the most important country in the hemisphere with which the United States does not have free trade. Consequently, other countries have rejected the trade sanctions approach, for the environment as well as labor. However, they have not rejected the idea of labor and environmental linkages in trade agreements, without forcing the trade negotiators themselves to deal with these issues except by reference to appropriate international organizations.

The key issue, therefore, is to reconcile diverse views, those internal to the United States in the first instance, in a way that does not preclude effective negotiation in the FTAA.

MODELS OF LABOR AND ENVIRONMENTAL ISSUES IN CURRENT TRADE AGREEMENTS

Following are some examples of how labor and environmental issues are dealt with in current trade agreements:

- The General Agreement on Tariffs and Trade (now the WTO) contains environmental provisions of a general nature that can be raised in trade disputes. No comparable labor provisions exist in the articles of the GATT (other than on the prohibition of prison labor).

- The U.S. general system of preferences (GSP) has trade penalties for infractions of core labor standards, but GSP is a unilateral benefit granted by the United States, not a negotiated one.

- Two side agreements exist in NAFTA: they contemplate possible trade sanctions (as between Mexico and the United States), but are so hemmed in that they are unlikely to be used.

- The Chile-Canada Free Trade Agreement and its side agreements permit fines against the country violating the labor and environmental provisions, and the funds are then added to the relevant budget of the offending country. They are, in essence, an internal government transfer mechanism.

- The Jordan-U.S. FTA contains labor and environmental provisions, in the basic agreement itself and states that, if a charge is upheld by an arbitration panel, the country bringing it is authorized to take "appropriate" countermeasures.

- Chile, in its current FTA negotiations with the United States, has stated its preference for side agreements on labor and the environment (a relatively minor point) and has added that it rejects trade sanctions (a major point); Chile has stated it would accept a system of fines similar to that that exists in the Chile-Canada FTA.

BRIDGING INTERNAL U.S. DISAGREEMENTS

Following are some ideas for bridging the internal U.S. disagreements that would permit hemispheric FTAA negotiations to proceed (the ideas are not mutually exclusive):

- Incorporate relevant international labor and environmental agreements into the FTAA by reference. This is done in NAFTA for the environmental agreements. The International Labor Organization (ILO) could (and should) be referenced in this manner as well in the FTAA.

- Set up a system of fines for countries that violate *their own* labor and environmental laws and regulations, with the understanding that the countries would pass these fines on to the offending corporations. In this way, fines would not be merely an internal government transfer from one part of the budget to another, but a penalty on violating companies, where they really belong. This would require transparency and the regular review of national laws and regulations and any changes in them. The fines against the offending country (and ultimately, the offending corporation) would be determined by an arbitration panel, based on specific guidelines. The arbitration panels would be best set up in the ILO.

- When the U.S. Congress authorized permanent normal trade relations for China, it also established a committee to review human rights issues in China. This model may be appropriate for labor and environmental issues in the FTAA when trade-promotion authority is granted. This would be internal to the United States, but it would provide a mechanism for the U.S. Congress to keep these issues under regular review and would enable Congress to comment publicly on them. This committee would be in addition to the labor and environmental provisions agreed to by all the countries.

CONCLUSION

The underlying premise of these suggestions is that continued head-on conflict between those groups that want labor and environmental provisions in any trade agreement and those groups that are equally adamant that these provisions are not appropriate to trade negotiations will lead to continued inaction on trade negotiations. The accompanying premise is that it is in the U.S. national interest to secure free trade in the Americas.

7 THE U.S. CONGRESS AND TRADE POLICY: GIVE ME A BREAK*

Those of us who work in Washington think tanks are asked regularly to interpret actions of the U.S. Congress to foreign and domestic journalists, businesspeople, government officials, and even to members of Congress and congressional staff. This is becoming near impossible when it comes to U.S. trade policy. I am repeatedly stumped by what Congress as a whole, or substantial segments of it, are doing—or think they are doing—on issue after issue. Consider the following.

1. *Late in the Clinton administration, in an agricultural appropriations bill, the Senate voted 86 to 8, with 6 abstentions, for an amendment introduced by Senator Robert Byrd (D-W.Va.) that provided for transferring funds obtained from antidumping and countervailing duty (AD and CVD) collections from the U.S. Treasury to the petitioning U.S. industries.* There was no previous congressional consideration of this amendment in the appropriations context, although similar legislation (the Continued Dumping and Subsidy Offset Act, or CDO) had been introduced two years earlier in both houses in the normal way, through the Finance and Ways and Means committees. President Clinton allowed the Byrd amendment to become law because he felt the appropriation was needed and the CDO aspect could be dealt with later. The Byrd amendment is still on books, and regulations for distributing the collections are scheduled to come into effect this fall. U.S. AD and CVD procedures have long been reviled by most U.S. trading partners for being protectionist, and the monetary incentive for companies to submit even more such petitions because of the Byrd amendment is obvious.

The steel industry is the biggest U.S. user of AD and CVD actions, and it surely is no coincidence that West Virginia has an important stake in steel production. We will probably find out if CDO distributions are compatible with the provisions of the World Trade Organization because, if they take place, many countries have stated they will contest them. If the U.S. action is not overturned, other countries will probably emulate the U.S. practice and start a subsidy war based on AD-CVD measures.

---

* *Issues in International Political Economy*, no. 19 (July 2001).

How can this action be explained? It was probably seen as an indirect way to subsidize steel production, plus a collection of other industries that use AD and CVD actions, without breaking the budget. Is this a worthy explanation? Senator Roth thought at the time that it was because it gave those parties injured by dumping double protection.

2. *Sixty-two senators signed a letter to President Bush, dated May 7, 2001, stating that changes in U.S. trade laws should not be on the table during international trade negotiations.* The immediate stimulus for the letter was Brazil's position that it saw little incentive to engage in negotiations for a Free Trade Area of the Americas if U.S. agricultural protection and AD-CVD actions were lodged in concrete. Brazil cited many U.S. import restrictions in defense of its position, such as those on orange juice and steel. The explicit assumption of the letter from the senators was that foreigners engage in "unfair trade practices," whereas U.S. laws, by contrast, promote free trade by countering these. The United States has not been hesitant in insisting that other countries change their laws to meet U.S. demands, which many did in the intellectual property negotiations in the Uruguay Round. One of the reasons for the failure of the Seattle ministerial meeting of the WTO in late 1999 was U.S. unwillingness to even consider changes in U.S. AD legislation and procedures.

Explanation? Perhaps the 62 senators are just trying to test the mettle of U.S. negotiators. Anybody can negotiate if benefits and obligations are reciprocal. It takes real skill to offer nothing as the quid pro quo for concessions from other countries.

3. *Congressman Phil Crane, chairman of the Subcommittee on Trade of the House Ways and Means Committee, submitted legislation last month to provide President Bush with trade-promotion authority (TPA) that takes no notice of labor and environmental safeguards in trade negotiations.* In the trade vernacular, this is a "clean" bill and the Republican leadership in the House supported it. The majority of Democrats in the House have made clear that they oppose TPA, which does not have labor and environmental provisions that, when violated, can be punished by trade restrictions. The Crane proposal, therefore, deliberately sets up a confrontation. The explanation offered by the defenders of the Crane proposal is that this is a way to get a "whip count" of support for a clean bill. This presumes that the Republican leadership cannot count

without specific legislation. Many in the business community who sincerely want trade negotiations are prepared to include labor and environmental issues in TPA as long as trade penalty sanctions are removed. The Bush administration itself has suggested a middle ground, one that uses a "toolbox" of carrots and sticks (such as fines, rather than trade penalties) to bridge the differences that exist.

Explanation? Many developing countries—India and Brazil are two important examples, but there are many others—have said they are unwilling to negotiate on trade with the United States if this entails accepting trade penalties for alleged labor and environmental infractions. Maybe the Republican leadership in the House wants to compete on equal terms with the majority of Democrats in the House. One group—the Democrats—wants TPA legislation that is non-negotiable with our trading partners, and the other—the Republican leadership—wants TPA legislation that is non-negotiable in the House of Representatives. Does either side want to negotiate?

4. *The House of Representatives passed a fiscal year 2002 transportation spending bill on June 26 that prohibits the use of funds to process applications by Mexico-domiciled motor carriers to operate outside commercial zones adjacent to the Mexico-U.S. border.* The amendment passed by a vote of 285 to 143. President Bush had said earlier that the U.S. government would comply with a NAFTA arbitration panel that, on February 6, 2001, ruled unanimously that the United States was in violation of its obligation in NAFTA to entertain applications from Mexican carriers to provide trucking services throughout the United States. The panel was made up of five arbitrators, two from the United States, two from Mexico, and one from Great Britain. President Bush has since stated that he will veto the House action.

NAFTA provided that trucking services from each country would be open to neighboring border states three years after the agreement was signed (i.e., as of December 18, 1995). The United States refused to implement this provision, citing safety concerns. NAFTA further provided that motor carriers domiciled in each country could petition to offer services anywhere in the other country six years after NAFTA went into effect (i.e., as of January 1, 2000). Again, the United States refused. To be more precise, the U.S. Department of Transportation (DOT), on safety grounds, refused to take applications from Mexican long-haul carriers. It has always been clear that each country—indeed, each U.S.

state—would enforce its own safety standards. The DOT, in a report on May 8, 2001, noted that the percentage of Mexican trucks out of service for safety reasons was considerably higher than for U.S. trucks, but that the out-of-service rate in California was about the same for trucks of each country in fiscal year 2000. The explanation was that California dedicated more inspectors at the border than did Texas, the main border-crossing point for U.S.-Mexico commerce. (Beyond this, the U.S. refusal to allow Mexican carriers to petition to invest in the United States was overturned; the arbitration panel said that the United States made no significant effort to defend this prohibition.)

Explanation? The Mexicans, in their presentation to the arbitration panel, cited political motives for the U.S. action, namely, the opposition of the Teamsters Union to long-haul Mexican trucks operating in the United States. The panel said it would not address this allegation, but instead dealt with the failure of the United States to grant Mexico national treatment under the provisions of NAFTA, and most-favored-nation treatment as compared with Canada. One explanation for the House vote—omitting any Teamster connection—is that because Congress found itself unable to punish the state from which the president comes for not taking action comparable to California, it decided instead to punish Mexico.

A final note: As is evident, I must be inventive in order to interpret many trade actions of Congress as being other than sheer protectionism. Maybe the explanation is that Congress is trying to test the imaginations of think-tankers.

8   A NEEDLESS TRADE WAR*

The economic press has characterized recent panel decisions on U.S. foreign sales corporations (FSCs) as having the wrecking potential of an atomic bomb on the World Trade Organization. In a definitive ruling released last month, the WTO appellate body affirmed that U.S. FSC legislation establishes a prohibited export subsidy. The decision opens the United States to retaliation that could amount to as much as $4 billion, which, if exercised by the European Union and other affected parties, could severely prejudice U.S. trade. This gigantic amount makes the war analogy so apt.

The appellate body ruling is steeped in legal language based on the wording of the WTO and the agreement on subsidies and countervailing measures. As I understand the reasoning of the appellate body, it would be consistent with the provisions of the WTO to subsidize exports to avoid double taxation if the exemption from U.S. taxes applied to income derived from foreign sources, which the FSC does not. Rather, it permits U.S. corporations to set up FSCs outside the United States and attribute the income to these essentially shell entities.

I am an economist, not a lawyer, and will therefore focus on the economic aspects of the FSC legislation. Indeed, the legal language derives from the underlying economic theory that prevailed when the General Agreement on Tariffs and Trade (the predecessor to the WTO) was established at the end of World War II. That theory, to put it simply, is that indirect taxes, such as value-added taxes and sales taxes, are passed forward to the ultimate consumer, whereas direct taxes, such as the income tax, are not, but instead are absorbed by the producer or seller of the good or service. In this construct, an indirect tax is best levied in the jurisdiction where the sale takes place. Taking this one step further, this means that indirect taxes paid before a good or service is exported can be reimbursed (a drawback can be claimed), leaving it up to the ultimate jurisdiction to apply the indirect taxes that prevail there. Direct taxes that are paid can have no drawback, which is why the U.S. Congress—responding to the urgings of large U.S. corporations—devised the FSC mechanism, and its gimmicky predecessor (the domestic international sales corporation, or DISC).

* *Issues in International Political Economy*, no. 26 (February 2002).

Today it is evident that this theory of tax incidence is much too simple. Some portion of income taxes surely is passed forward and the seller may absorb some portion of indirect taxes. When this was pointed out as long ago as the 1960s, the argument of many of the experts, including those from the European Commission, was that the issue was being overblown by the United States because shifts in exchange rates—especially under a floating system, such as that which now exists between the dollar and the euro—largely neutralizes these tax incidence distinctions.

This reasoning—that exchange-rate shifts made the economic theory underlying the export drawback rules, even if not airtight, largely irrelevant—did not prevent the European Commission from belatedly launching a case against the United States about the FSC many years after its enactment. The commissioner who spearheaded this action, Leon Brittan, recently wrote a letter to the *Financial Times* (January 16, 2002) to deny the charge that this was done in a fit of pique over U.S. action against EU banana policy. The letter has a sanctimonious tone that the issue had to be pursued in the WTO "in order to protect legitimate commercial interests of EU businesses." The *Wall Street Journal* took an opposite but equally self-serving position when it argued in an editorial (on January 17, 2002) that the FSC case was not about trade, but rather about taxes in the sense that rebates of Europe's value-added taxes were needed in order to make Europe competitive in world markets.

We now have the makings of the mother of all trade wars between the European Union and the United States on an issue on which both sides have little to be proud of and that could seriously damage the WTO. The U.S. Congress deliberately sought a way to subsidize exports by massaging the rules of the GATT, an agreement that U.S. trade and legal experts largely wrote; and the European Commission went looking for a fight that would give it some leverage in bargaining on other issues. (Lord Brittan's letter makes this clear when he suggests that one U.S. concession might be to reduce its "extremely high tariffs on textiles.")

The real issue is where the two sides go from here. One possibility is that, after the legal experts at the WTO decide on the precise amount of damage, the EU can retaliate by raising tariffs or imposing other import restrictions for the full amount. This would be a declaration of war and, in my view, irresponsible. More likely, a mix of actions—EU import restrictions and U.S. concessions—will be worked out. Even this can be obviated if the U.S. Congress alters the legislation in a way that conforms to the guidance given by the appellate body, but this would not be easy to accomplish. U.S. trade officials are also talking about changing the rules about direct and indirect taxes embodied in the WTO, but given the EU preference for the current provisions, this would be an impossible negotiation. The United States can respond by bringing a series of charges against the EU; the *Wall Street Journal* editorial suggested a complaint over Europe's subsidies to Airbus. This is advice to escalate the trade war by bringing in other issues.

This listing of options to resolve the dispute makes it clear that there is no easy solution. We are in a fight that the United States should not have started by instituting the FSC in the first place, and that the EU should not have pursued at this late date. This fight between the world's two largest trading entities is made to order for philosophizing about how the international trading system works.

The GATT and the WTO today establish a body of rules, something that is necessary to the conduct of trade among nations. The rules, for the most part, are based on the common-sense principle that countries should not seek special advantages to further their exports that are not available to all other members of the trading regime. This most-favored-nation principle is then encrusted with exceptions, the most prominent of which is the authority to establish customs unions and free-trade areas under a separate set of rules. By now, these preferential arrangements are the vehicles for more trade than the MFN rule itself.

It is well known in trade-policy circles that many countries make a concerted effort to keep their exchange rates slightly undervalued in order to promote exports. There is a downside to this practice in that it can have an inflationary impact, but not an excessive one if the undervaluation is modest. It is tempting to game the rules in order to give one's exporters an advantage, no matter how slight. Rules are fine, but getting around the rules is even more exhilarating.

The FSC idea was premised on getting around the rules. It was an attempt by U.S. corporations to equalize the competitive impact of different tax systems on international trade. The United States relies more on the corporate income tax to raise revenue than it does on value-added taxes, whereas the EU relies heavily on the VAT. When the FSC and its predecessor were concocted, the argument made by U.S. corporations was that they were seeking only to correct an injustice written into the

GATT articles that favored corporations in countries that relied heavily on indirect taxes. Now that the FSC has run afoul of those who interpret the international trade rules, it is likely that there will be a concerted corporate drive to change U.S. tax laws to reduce reliance on income taxes and move instead to value-added or other indirect taxes. It will not matter that the trade impact of such a change might not be significant over time as relative exchange rates adjust under a floating system.

The concern aroused by the ruling of the appellate body was that a U.S.-EU trade war over the FSC would damage the World Trade Organization. We may discover that there is another concern here in the United States—that this ruling, based on the wording of the WTO and related trade agreements, will serve as the basis for changing the nature of the U.S. tax system itself. This, if it takes place, will require time and much bloody argumentation, but there already are a number of proposals out there to take advantage of the WTO ruling in order to make the U.S. tax system more hospitable to international trade rules rather than to tax progressivity. Representative Bill Thomas (R-Cal.), chairman of the House Ways and Means Committee, is among those who would like to use the WTO ruling to overhaul the U.S. tax system.

9   THE ELUSIVE OPTION TO OPEN MARKETS*

Many commentators from the region question the validity of open markets in Latin America and the Caribbean, especially now after Argentina's financial and economic collapse. Their reasoning is straightforward, even if simplistic: economic growth in the 1990s—the first full decade after import markets were broadly opened—was meager in most countries. The recommendation that flowed from this observation was that open market policies should be jettisoned. It is rarely specified what should replace them.

Eduardo Duhalde, when he was chosen as the president of Argentina on January 1, 2002, was an exception. He stated his belief that the open import market was destroying Argentine industry and he advocated a reversion to nationalistic protection. (In fact, Argentina's import market was not that open; the average tariff was 13.5 percent, one of the highest in Latin America.) He was correct in his assertion that Argentine industry is, by and large, noncompetitive, but this is more the result of an overvalued exchange rate over many years than an open market. Duhalde could have looked across the Andes to observe that Chile had lower import tariffs, fewer nontariff gimmicks to impede imports, a flexible exchange rate, and rigorous macroeconomic policies—and was enjoying steady economic growth. Chile was demonstrating that the problem was not the liberal economic model, but rather the way policy is carried out. Duhalde has since backed away from his initial comments on augmenting Argentina's import protection.

There has been little economic fallout elsewhere in Latin America from the Argentine disaster. This led to a contagion argument with a slightly different nuance, that there would be an adverse *political* reaction across the hemisphere to the kind of "open" market policy that Argentina practiced. The reasoning is that the first requirement of a political leader is to stay alive, and the Argentine case demonstrated that this might not be possible in a democracy that practiced liberal economic policies. The logic of this approach is somewhat more sophisticated than the straightforward economic argument, but it is based on the special situation in one country.

* *Issues in International Political Economy*, no. 29 (May 2002).

The liberal development model adopted almost across the board in Latin America arose from the disastrous experience of the hemisphere in the 1980s. The Mexican economy collapsed at the end of 1982, and a chain reaction that altered the previous model of import substitution followed across most of the hemisphere. The 1980s were justly referred to in the hemisphere as the "lost decade." Annual GDP growth in that decade in Latin America and the Caribbean averaged 1 percent. In addition, officials in most countries realized that they had built up unsupportable debt even as they were saddled with industries largely unable to compete internationally, let alone in their home markets. It was evident to policymakers within the region that there was no return to the status quo ante—not then, not now.

The shift in the economic model was led by Chile during the Pinochet dictatorship. Chile suffered a major economic collapse in 1982, when GDP fell by 14 percent, but the corrective was to alter elements of the liberal model (such as exchange-rate policy) without changing its basic thrust—and the Chilean economy has prospered ever since. GDP grew by an annual average of more than 5 percent in the 15 years since 1986, by which time the effects of the 1982 crisis had been resolved. When democracy returned to Chile in 1990, the *concertación* (the alliance of parties that won the presidency) promised in their electoral campaign that the new government would essentially follow the liberal macroeconomic model put in place by Pinochet's economic team. And democratic Chile did exactly that, even as it added safeguards for labor and other embellishments to the program inherited from the dictatorship.

Mexico, whose inability to service foreign debt set off the hemisphere's debt crisis of the 1980s, followed the economic example of Chile and began in the mid-1980s to unilaterally open its import market. This culminated, if that is the right word, with the initiative to enter into free trade with the United States and Canada. (The word "culminated" is troublesome because NAFTA, in reality, was the beginning of a process of North American economic integration.) Brazil and Argentina adopted a similar policy focused on southern integration, one that led to the creation of Mercosur. This "common market of the south" has had its problems, but all of the four member countries (Argentina, Brazil, Paraguay, and Uruguay) hope to be able to resolve these in the future.

The practice throughout the hemisphere—in Chile, Mexico, Brazil, Argentina, and elsewhere—was to unilaterally reduce import barriers, that is, without seeking reciprocity, in the belief that lower-cost imports encouraged more competitive exports. After agreement was reached at the Miami Summit in 1994 for a free-trade area covering the entire hemisphere, unilateral import tariff reductions ceased; countries felt they had to conserve their bargaining chips for a negotiation with the United States that would entail reciprocity.

Another near-universal pattern emerged as hemispheric countries had to confront economic crises. Instead of changing the model, as many critics of "neoliberalism" advocated, policymakers tended to deepen the open market model. This is what happened in Chile after the 1982 crisis, in Mexico after the 1994 crisis, and in Brazil in 1999.

There are many reasons for this. The most important is that there is no evident viable alternative. Most hemispheric countries are too small to look exclusively inward for their economic stimulus. Many are concluding free-trade agreements to enlarge the potential size of markets, but this is also limiting. Chile is seeking a free-trade agreement with the United States in order to attract more foreign investment. The Central American countries were elated when President Bush indicated the intention of the United States to seek free trade with them. The only hemispheric country that has an internal market large enough to practice import substitution on a reasonable scale is Brazil, but Brazil's deeper interest is to expand its exports globally.

Under these circumstances, the option between open markets and protectionism is a non-choice. It is open markets or acceptance of slow growth. This does not mean that the liberal model has to be identical in all countries. The export potential differs by country. Countries do not privatize to the same extent. The large countries now have floating exchange rates, but others may wish to dollarize. But no country in the hemisphere rejects the reality of globalization and the need to attract direct investment and expand its exports. No hemispheric country has rejected the idea of hemispheric free trade. Some may prefer to give higher priority to global negotiations, other to subregional agreements, and others to the hemispheric initiative. Some countries—Brazil predominantly—are skeptical that the United States is fully prepared to open its market. Even so, this does not negate the need for open markets; it only serves to underscore the difficulty of achieving them.

There may be talk of a model change—but, so far, it is largely talk by critics not responsible for making day-to-day economic policy in hemispheric countries. There will surely be continued political fallout if economic growth rates do not improve, but few leaders are able to come up with model changes that will improve the situation. If recent experience is any guide, the leaders are more likely to see their solution in opening their markets even more in various forms of trade negotiations.

10 HISTORY REPEATS ITSELF IN TRADE POLICY*

Current U.S. practice in negotiating trade agreements is roughly as follows: When negotiating globally on a variety of trade issues, the preferred forum is the World Trade Organization, where the benefits and obligations undertaken are on a most-favored-nation basis; when negotiating globally in a single functional area, the WTO is also the preferred forum, again on an MFN basis, but these negotiations can be pursued without trade-promotion authority (TPA); the U.S. government is also prepared to negotiate regionally for free trade (i.e., on a discriminatory basis, also with TPA); finally, the government is prepared to conclude free-trade agreements, sometimes with TPA and sometimes without, with individual countries or groups of countries. The Doha Round is the global WTO negotiation; telecommunications negotiations were undertaken in the WTO without TPA; the Free Trade Area of the Americas is the current regional negotiation; and bilateral and plurilateral negotiations include those with Jordan, Chile, Singapore, and the countries of the Central American Common Market. The prototype of regional free trade for the United States is the North American Free Trade Agreement.

The decision to proceed with the NAFTA negotiations was made in the midst of lagging Uruguay Round negotiations, although not without some controversy within the U.S. government, and this turned out to stimulate the global negotiations. This experience was then transformed into a philosophy, that FTAs are stepping-stones to more productive global negotiations. Not everybody agrees with this thinking; there is strong sentiment that this division of the world into competing discriminatory arrangements distorts rather than encourages an efficient and just world trading system. The evidence thus far is insufficient to determine which view—the stepping-stone or the stumbling-block hypothesis—is correct.

What is uncanny, however, is how policy experiments repeat themselves periodically in different guises. Initial trade policy, when the United States became an independent country, took the form of conditional MFN, namely, that concessions granted in a bilateral trade agreement with one country would be granted to another country only

---

* *Issues in International Political Economy*, no. 34 (October 2002).

on the condition that a separate bilateral agreement with its own benefits for the United States was concluded. This policy broke down in the 1920s, after the United States became an important world trader, because it became an impediment to good political relations. Countries facing discrimination in the U.S. market could obtain equal treatment only by concluding a separate agreement, something that led to interminable negotiations. In addition, not all countries could grant the reciprocal benefits necessary to acquire the same treatment as that granted in the original agreement. This led to the shift from conditional to unconditional MFN (i.e., treating all countries alike, or what in more recent legislation is called normal trade relations).

Later, in the 1930s, under the reciprocal trade agreements program sponsored by Secretary of State Cordell Hull, the new unconditional MFN policy took the form of a series of bilateral trade agreements. The main purpose of this program was to reduce the protectionism that dominated U.S. trade policy under the Smoot-Hawley legislation. This was a retail way of opening markets, doing it country by country. When GATT was created in the immediate postwar period, the inefficiency of retail trade liberalization became manifest, and the new technique born at that time was to reduce trade barriers, mostly tariffs at first, in rounds of multilateral trade negotiations. The first article of the GATT contains the MFN principle, although the exceptions allowed for customs unions and free-trade areas have now become commonplace.

When a bilateral or regional free-trade agreement is concluded, the benefits are granted only to the countries included in the negotiation; all other countries face discrimination, unless they can conclude separate FTAs with the United States. The only difference between this and the pre-1920s policy is that the conditional nature relates now to free trade rather than to MFN treatment. Arguably, there is another difference in that tariffs today are lower than they were in the 1920s, but discrimination is there nevertheless. In addition, there are many fierce and highly protective nontariff barriers today, and most of these are eliminated in FTAs.

After NAFTA was concluded, the United States found it politically necessary to provide some compensatory relief to countries in Central America and the Caribbean that faced discrimination, as compared with Mexico, and this took the form of special trade preferences for them. Something similar was done for the Andean countries. One preference almost inevitably leads to another and another and another.

The members of Mercosur (Brazil, Argentina, Paraguay, and Uruguay) often call our attention to the fact that they are just about the only hemispheric countries not getting preferential treatment in the U.S. market. Their point is a political one: what have they done to deserve this discriminatory treatment? In a recent talk in Washington, the president of the Dominican Republic, pointing to the prospective U.S. free-trade negotiations with Central America, said this would damage his country; he also wanted an FTA with the United States.

When the FTA with Singapore is completed, other countries in Asia are sure to ask why they are facing discrimination. The likely outcome will be a plea for separate FTAs of their own with the United States or, alternatively, FTAs among themselves discriminating against U.S. products (see below). Australia has already indicated that it wants an FTA with the United States but is meeting considerable resistance from the U.S. government because of the importance of agricultural products in its export mix. This unequal trade treatment may turn a solid ally into a reluctant cooperator. My prediction is that, in time, this political reality will force us into some kind of free trade with Australia and New Zealand.

When the FTAA comes into existence, assuming that it does, this could stimulate several outcomes. One is that Asian countries will reach their own discriminatory arrangements against products coming from the United States and set up pressure for U.S. exporters to take some corrective action. The other is that the United States, or perhaps FTAA countries generally, will seek to eliminate the counterdiscrimination each faces in the other's markets by opening cross-Pacific free-trade discussions. Conditional free trade is no more stable, over time, than was conditional MFN.

It is also evident that one path the United States is following today is retail free trade. Mexico first, then Central America, tomorrow the Dominican Republic? Today the Andean Group, tomorrow Mercosur? Today Chile, then what? A U.S.-Chile FTA has been in the making for so long that it really must succeed this time or the relationship will become strained. For the United States, if an FTA cannot be concluded with Chile, then the FTAA itself becomes a questionable exercise. Chile has thus become a test case for hemispheric free trade.

Few analysts of trade policy quarrel with the proposition that global trade liberalization is the optimal outcome, certainly for industrial countries. A closed European Union, or a closed free-trade area in the

Western Hemisphere, would be a catastrophe. The argument thus rests on the stepping-stone/stumbling-block outcome. Will the existence of discriminatory groupings in Europe, the Western Hemisphere, and potentially large parts of Asia be durable or lead to negotiation to end this hemispheric discrimination? Will the problems created by conditional free trade, which must be retail because conditional means omitting countries until later, break down as a result of political annoyances?

The attractiveness of the FTAA is that it can cut through the spaghetti bowl arrangements that now typify Latin American and Caribbean trade and eliminate most of the cross preferences (differential discrimination) created by the 20 or more FTA agreements that exist. The FTAA, of course, creates its own problems with the rest of the world. Nevertheless, there is little doubt that a negotiation to liberalize hemispheric trade can be more comprehensive today (except perhaps in agriculture) than a negotiation seeking global liberalization. But we should be clear: We are buying an unstable situation that will create problems and need correction over time.

I doubt that U.S. officials who make trade policy think at all about how politically complex it became to retain conditional MFN. They surely are becoming aware of the complexity of conditional free trade, but presumably conclude that this is a problem for later; for now, the issue is to benefit U.S. exporters. But a monster has been unleashed, and other countries have been more adept at concluding FTAs than the United States. It is not clear that we are taming this monster by leaping head first ourselves into serial FTAs of our own, particularly bilateral or plurilateral FTAs, as opposed to regional (the Western Hemisphere) or global trade liberalization.

11 LACK OF CLARITY IN U.S. TRADE POLICY[*]

For those who believe that international trade increases world economic welfare, the best negotiating forum for reaching trade deals has to be the global one, the World Trade Organization. Its importance also explains why the WTO is anathema to trade and globalization skeptics. There is considerable disagreement among analysts as to whether nonglobal trade agreements also stimulate total trade, but few analysts contend that they can substitute for global negotiations. The stimulus contention is that more comprehensive commitments can be negotiated in smaller negotiations. The North American Free Trade Agreement—NAFTA—went much further in liberalizing trade and investment rights and obligations among the three countries of North America than would have been possible in the Uruguay Round then under negotiation in the General Agreement on Tariffs and Trade; and some of these advances were later incorporated in the final Uruguay Round agreement. The downside of these smaller free-trade agreements is that they discriminate against countries not party to them. They therefore negate the most important principle of the WTO, that of most-favored-nation (nondiscriminatory) treatment. This much is common knowledge among trade policy experts.

Robert Zoellick, the U.S. trade representative, has enunciated a strategy that he calls "competitive liberalization." He laid out his thinking in a recent *Wall Street Journal* article (July 10, 2003). What this competition means in practice is that the United States will negotiate reductions in trade barriers simultaneously in a variety of forums—bilateral, plurilateral, regional, and global. Bilateral free-trade negotiations were just completed with Chile and Singapore; plurilateral free-trade negotiations are taking place with the five countries of the Central American Common Market; regional negotiations are in progress to establish a free-trade area of the Americas, or FTAA; and the WTO will have a ministerial meeting in Cancun, Mexico, from September 10 to 14, to assess progress in the ongoing Doha Round.

It is by no means clear how the United States chooses its bilateral negotiating partners—and many are in the wings. The General Accounting Office, at the request of Senator Max Baucus (D-Mont.), is now

[*] *Issues in International Political Economy*, no. 43 (July 2003).

engaged in a study to clarify this. Sometimes the choice is based mainly on the open trade policy of the partner countries (like Chile and Singapore), sometimes on hemispheric political grounds (as with Central America), sometimes on global strategy (as in the proposed negotiations in the Middle East), and sometimes because of support for U.S. foreign policy (hence Australia "yes," New Zealand "no").

Keep in mind that the main justification for nonglobal negotiations is that more can be achieved in them than in a WTO exercise. Yet, the current indication coming out of Washington is that the FTAA will be slimmed down in substance to meet misgivings of other hemispheric countries. It is becoming more clear daily that the Central American agreement is likely to be a watered-down version of the Chile and Singapore free trade agreements (FTAs). This leaves the uneasy feeling that reaching agreement takes priority over the content.

The United States took the issue of agricultural subsidies off the table in the FTAA negotiations on the ground that this was the wrong forum for getting reciprocal subsidy reductions from the European Union and Japan. These negotiations would therefore be reserved for the WTO. The United States said much the same thing about changes in antidumping and countervailing duty laws and procedures—that, in the unlikely event any changes were made in these unfair trade practices, this would have to take place in the WTO where reciprocity would be global. The Brazilians then suggested, because agricultural subsidies are important to them, that intellectual property protection should also be removed from the FTAA discussions. Subsequent indications are that many hemispheric countries would like to limit the scope of the FTAA negotiations in trade in services, government procurement, and investment promotion. The implication of all this is that the FTAA may turn out to be a negotiation on market access—an important subject, but only part of what the United States insisted on when negotiating with Chile—and all of the rest can then be deferred to the WTO negotiation. Trade policy analysts used to talk about regional and bilateral agreements as being "WTO-plus." We are now prepared to make them WTO-minus and to make the WTO negotiation a sort of FTAA-plus.

Another complaint about U.S. trade policy is coming from the business community, namely, that the plethora of trade agreements recently negotiated and being contemplated do not involve very much trade. Chile and Singapore are important markets for the United States (U.S. exports to these countries in 2002 were $2.6 billion and $16.2 billion respectively), but they pale in comparison with Canada and Mexico

($160 billion and $97.5 billion last year). U.S. exports to Jordan ($404 million in 2002), with which an FTA exists, are clearly underwhelming, as are our merchandise shipments to Morocco ($565 million in 2002) and Bahrain ($419 million last year), with which FTA negotiations are contemplated. According to *Business Week* (July 7, 2003), many leading business groups have expressed their dismay. They apparently prefer that trade agreements be used to promote trade rather than as political tools.

The plethora of FTAs also complicates the operations of U.S. corporations in other ways. Each agreement has its own rules of origin,[1] and corporations must keep track of these differences as they multiply, agreement by agreement. The same product may qualify for export to one destination, but not to others. For example, U.S. corporations took advantage of the rules set up for textile trade with Central America by shipping U.S. fabric to Honduras and then discovered that the resulting product, although it met the rule of origin for shipment to the United States, could not enter duty-free into Mexico under the rules of origin in the Honduras-Mexico agreement.

There is always a political element in a trade negotiation, especially because an FTA provides a preferential benefit not generally available to other countries. The elder President Bush undoubtedly welcomed Mexico's request in the early 1990s to negotiate an FTA with the United States because it signaled a positive shift in the relationship, but—and this must be emphasized—also held the potential for significant trade and investment expansion. The proposal for free trade in the Americas has a large political element in light of where the United States is located, but the idea is not merely symbolic because trade and investment consequences can be substantial. However, current U.S. policy seems to put a more direct emphasis on the political aspects of trade agreements. The signing of the Chile FTA was delayed briefly because of U.S. unhappiness over Chile's opposition to the second United Nations resolution on war with Iraq. The *Financial Times* (June 30, 2003) reported that the United States suspended free-trade talks with Egypt after that country reversed its agreement to cosponsor the U.S. complaint to the WTO against the European Union for its refusal to allow genetically modified foods to be imported. Egypt apparently took this action because the EU takes 40 percent of its exports.

The sense that is now being conveyed around the world is that U.S. policy is to sign FTAs with other countries only if those countries are prepared to adhere to U.S. foreign policy positions. An FTA, in other words, is not necessarily an agreement in which all parties benefit from trade expansion, but rather a favor to be bestowed based on support of U.S. foreign policy.

There are pluses to concluding an FTAA "lite," if this is the only way to save the agreement. An agreement on market access could substantially lower import barriers of key Latin American countries, especially Brazil. A market access agreement including most Latin American and Caribbean countries would encourage trade among them on an equal basis and could simplify the rules of origin if most existing FTAs in the hemisphere were folded into the FTAA with a single set of rules. There are also minuses: a watered-down FTAA would weaken the U.S. discipline of concluding preferential agreements only if they are WTO-plus; and in the process, this would further downgrade the WTO as the negotiating forum of choice.

Note

[1] These rules set forth the criteria that products must meet to be eligible for free trade, such as how much production took place in the exporting country. These rules are necessary in a free trade area in order to prevent export of a product to a low-tariff member of an FTA for subsequent transshipment to a higher-tariff member.

12 TRADE NEGOTIATION PROSPECTS: GLOBAL AND HEMISPHERIC*

The failure of the ministerial trade meeting in Cancún in September 2003 was a serious blow to the further liberalization of world trade in goods and services. The other ongoing big trade negotiation involving the United States is to establish a Free Trade Area of the Americas designed to include all countries in the hemisphere, save Cuba. Both the Doha Round, for which the Cancún meeting was a mid-point stocktaking, and the FTAA have scheduled termination dates for the end of 2004. The next stocktaking meeting for the FTAA will be in Miami next month. There is considerable doubt that either negotiation can be concluded by the designated deadline, or be concluded at all—ever. This commentary will deal with the connection between these two negotiations.

The feature of the Cancún meeting that attracted considerable commentary was the united position of a Group of 20 countries, enlarged at some points and diminished at others—the Group of 20+, led by Brazil, India, China, and South Africa. The Group of 20+ focused initially on agricultural issues, mainly to reduce and eventually eliminate domestic and export subsidies in the industrial countries (the United States, the European Union, and Japan). This later expanded into the refusal of many of the G-20+ to deal at all with four issues left over from an earlier meeting in Singapore (the Singapore issues) concerning negotiation on investment, competition policy, transparency in government procurement, and trade facilitation. It is impossible to state which issue was responsible for the stalemate at Cancún—agriculture; the Singapore issues; the insistence of four African countries on the elimination of rich-country subsidies to produce cotton, coupled with a request for compensation for past damage done to them—in that all were part of the process.

The developing countries have joined together previously, particularly the formation of the so-called Group of 77 in the United Nations Conference on Trade and Development in the 1960s to establish a New International Economic Order (NIEO). The developing-country urge to

---

* *Issues in International Political Economy*, no. 46 (October 2003).

unite in order to exert countervailing leverage in economic dealings with the industrial countries is natural and eminently understandable. But it can also be destructive of accomplishment in so far as confrontation that does not abate at the proper moment leads to rigidity in position rather than to compromise. The Cancún rigidity is potentially much more serious than was that of the NIEO because the World Trade Organization is an active negotiating body and not a debating organization. The loss of world growth that a failure of the Doha Round would signify would affect the developing countries more adversely than it would the rich countries.

Casting blame for the collapse of the Cancún meeting is an empty exercise; there is blame enough to cover all the key participants. The real issue is what, if anything, can be done to relaunch the Doha Round. The WTO secretariat is actively exploring this prospect. The pressure on agricultural issues in Cancún did provoke some movement in the entrenched subsidy policies of the EU and the United States, but not enough to rescue the meeting before time ran out. There was some indication at Cancún that the EU was prepared to drop its insistence on negotiating the first two Singapore issues (investment and competition policies). There was progress at Cancún on other important issues, such as trade in services. In other words, there is some prospect that the Doha Round negotiation can start again where the Cancún meeting left off, and perhaps without the bitter confrontation.

However, there is considerable concern among trade negotiators in the industrial countries that the WTO may be too large (146 member countries) to continue to work under a rule of consensus for making decisions. The reality is that only a handful of countries (counting the EU as a single negotiator) carry out the bulk of world trade and are impeded in their negotiations by an unwieldy WTO. In the past, there was a process under which informal give-and-take took place in smaller groups whose decisions were then largely adopted by the membership as a whole, but this broke down in Cancún. This is the second spectacular failure of a WTO ministerial meeting in just a few years (the first was the Seattle meeting in 1999). Not only may it prove impossible to conduct the Doha Round negotiations under the old procedures, but it would take time to agree on changes in the decisionmaking process and still meet the year-end 2004 deadline. In either case, the Doha Round negotiations may be suspended for years, or forever, in favor of a new trade negotiating technique.

I am not clued in well enough on the thinking of key countries to make a sound prediction as to which outcome will prevail—whether a new beginning based on what has been accomplished so far in the Doha Round negotiations can be fashioned (an optimistic scenario from my viewpoint) or whether the new beginning will be to the entire process that has marked postwar multilateral trade negotiations up to this point.

Turning to the FTAA, the future is equally murky. The following are some of the considerations at play here: Most hemispheric countries want an FTAA; or, failing that, a bilateral free-trade agreement with the United States. The problem with the bilateral approach is that it does not liberalize trade among all (or most) hemispheric countries under the same rules. It does not deal effectively with south-south trade. A series of bilateral FTAs with the United States and between hemispheric countries also loses the spirit of cohesion in the hemisphere that the FTAA would represent.

Venezuela under President Hugo Chávez is against any trade agreement that includes the United States; he has indicated that he would like some association with Mercosur. The trouble with this is that Venezuela's export market is in the United States, not in the Southern Cone of Latin America. In practice, therefore, Venezuela can be ignored in calculations about the FTAA as long as Chávez is in power.

The resistance of Brazil to a comprehensive FTAA, on the other hand, is a significant consideration. Brazil reiterated as recently as early October at an FTAA meeting in Trinidad that it prefers that certain themes be omitted from the negotiations, such as intellectual property and government procurement. Brazil has not indicated what it is prepared to negotiate on services. One Brazilian argument is that if the United States can exclude farm subsidies and antidumping duties, Brazil can do the same for its sensitive themes. Taking their cue from Brazil, a number of other hemispheric countries have indicated that they would prefer to limit negotiation in areas that are sensitive for them. The U.S. business community—the large multinational enterprises—has made clear in a letter to the U.S. trade representative and the secretary of commerce that it would not support an FTAA "lite." The differences in these two viewpoints can be put more starkly: Brazil proposes an FTAA of the type that would not be supported in the United States. This, then, becomes meaningless. The most important market for the bulk of hemispheric countries is the United States.

Is the FTAA still feasible in light of what happened in Cancún? The United States is unwilling to discuss modification of its farm subsidies in a hemispheric meeting where comparable concessions cannot be extracted from the EU or Japan. Nor is the United States prepared to discuss modification of its unfair trade procedures in a regional meeting—and perhaps not really in a global meeting either. This, plus the position of Brazil, would lead one to conclude that the FTAA will fail.

However, there is another way of looking at the prospects of the FTAA. Before Cancún, hemispheric countries could hold back from making commitments about FTAA negotiations in the belief that most issues would be addressed in the Doha Round. This second option is now doubtful. For hemispheric countries, therefore, the only trade games in town are the FTAA or bilateral FTAs with the United States. This will certainly be the context at the Miami FTAA meeting. This would lead one to suspect that the breakdown at Cancún makes it more likely that the FTAA will come to fruition. This is my assessment—that the Cancún failure has improved the chances for making progress in the FTAA.

The Miami ministerial meeting of the FTAA can be viewed as stock-taking similar to that in Cancún for the Doha Round—to assess where the countries are in the negotiations and what must be done to conclude the negotiations by year-end 2004. It would be a double blow if the Miami meeting ended as did the Cancún meeting. I have asked myself how I would play the Miami meeting if I were the U.S. trade representative. Here are some thoughts.

- Because just about all countries in the hemisphere want an FTAA in order to provide greater assurance of access to the U.S. market, I would stand firm on a comprehensive agreement to be completed by the deadline. I would want Brazil to agree with this position, but if it does not, then so be it. There can be an FTAA without Brazil. There already is much criticism within Brazil of the stance Itamaraty (the Brazilian Foreign Ministry) took in Trinidad. Even the two smaller Mercosur partners implied they are ready to break ranks with Brazil. Brazil's only allies in the hemisphere would be Venezuela and—perhaps—Argentina. An FTAA without Brazil would not be optimal, but better than a complete collapse of the FTAA process.

- At the same time, there should be no desire to punish or isolate Brazil any more than it isolates itself. Brazil has its own important market access issues with the United States other than agriculture, and these can be addressed effectively in the FTAA. The United States should also commit itself to renew the agricultural subsidy issue from where it stood at Cancún when and if the Doha Round proceeds. For all practical purposes, this commitment is already implicit.

- A somewhat more radical step the United States can take in the FTAA is to support the idea of making the Western Hemisphere a zone free of agricultural export subsidies. Other hemispheric countries have already suggested this. The implication is that EU agricultural export subsidies would face countervailing duties on goods shipped to the Western Hemisphere. I am unable to speak to the legality of such a measure in the context of WTO commitments, but it may be permissible in the ambit of a free trade area.

I come to one other conclusion, namely, that progress in the FTAA would stimulate progress in the Doha Round. My reasoning is that the EU and Japan would want to minimize the discrimination they would face in a Western Hemisphere linked by the FTAA, and are likely to want to reduce the degree of this discrimination by reducing the hemisphere's general tariff level.

PART TWO

ECONOMIC POLICY

The last four years, the period covered by the essays in this book, have not been felicitous economically. There was little growth in most countries in Latin America and the Caribbean (LAC) and stagnation as well in the United States, Western Europe, and Japan. In addition, there have been some spectacular economic-financial collapses in LAC countries. The Argentine economy self-destructed in slow motion with many years of recession followed by a complete economic breakdown in 2002. Although Argentina's economic problems had been building up over many years, the precipitating event for the collapse was the decision to end the convertibility program of one Argentine peso equaling one U.S. dollar early in 2002. There were signs of recovery in 2003, but Argentina's economic prospects remain highly uncertain. So does its political future, which depends heavily on the accomplishments of its recently elected president, Néstor Kirchner.

Brazil felt it necessary to devalue its currency, the *real*, early in 1999, but its growth since then has been modest. The direction of the Brazilian economy is now in the hands of its Labor Party president, Luis Inácio "Lula" da Silva, who won the presidency in his fourth try in 2002. The change in the political direction of the presidency was even more spectacular in Mexico when Vicente Fox won election in 2000, altering the party of the president for the first time in 71 years. Unfortunately, Fox's administration thus far has had little economic success; Mexico, like Brazil, has experienced low economic growth for the past several years.

For LAC as a whole, per capita gross domestic product declined during the 1980s, recovered somewhat in the first half of the 1990s, and then fell into stagnation and decline again toward the end of the 1990s and into the present century. There were exceptions. The most important was Chile, which grew spectacularly in the latter half of the 1980s and well into the 1990s. Chile is still performing better than the remainder of LAC, although the torrid pace of its growth has slowed from what it was in the 15 previous heyday years.

The poor economic performance of most of LAC over the past 20-plus years has brought much disillusion with the economic model that went into effect during the debt-ridden decade of the 1980s. There is much questioning today in LAC as to whether the current liberal economic model is appropriate for it. Criticism abounds about what the critics call the "neoliberal" model of development, one that entails open markets, privatization of previously government-owned enterprises, and severe fiscal and monetary discipline. The elements of the model have come to be known as the "Washington consensus," a name given by the economist John Williamson to a series of requirements that included the foregoing policies. The Washington consensus may be dead, as many LAC critics aver, but nothing concrete has been suggested about what should replace it. Reversion to import substitution is not realistic. A return to inflation coming from large fiscal deficits is not desired by the bulk of the LAC population. The return of repetitive currency devaluations is not a rational outcome.

What is most likely, if growth is not soon restored, are changes at the margin—perhaps some deprivatization, maybe some modestly additional import protection for sensitive products, and other comparable measures. There are, of course, other options, such as the economically disastrous path President Hugo Chávez is pursuing in Venezuela. He is focusing instead on erasing all viable political opposition. LAC countries, now that they have entered the world marketplace and seek ever-larger amounts of capital inflows, especially foreign direct investment, can no longer look inwardly for economic stimulus. LAC countries also have a difficult time practicing countercyclical fiscal policy—that is, running deficits to stimulate the economy during a downturn. If they sought to do this, the capital inflows that they require to sustain investment would slow or even cease. They do not have the luxury of running large budget deficits, as the United States is doing. Only two countries in the region—Chile and Mexico—have been able to practice short-run countercyclical policy, and this is because they built up foreign reserves to tide them over the rough period.

Another tendency in the region is for politicians and intellectual organizers to blame the rest of the world for their situation. This takes the form of railing against globalization and powerful multinational corporations (which may be the same thing), criticizing the Washington consensus, and berating international institutions such as the World Trade Organization, the International Monetary Fund, and even the World Bank for the way they work. Some of the criticism may be valid, but few constructive options are proposed. Consequently, there have been few significant changes in the development model. It is also evident that the liberal economic model can work; the experience of Chile demonstrates this. However, the discipline that Chile has shown is not easily replicated in the rest of the region.

It would make an enormous difference to the economic prospects of LAC if the United States could resume its role as the main engine of growth in the Americas. If higher GDP growth could also be attained in European Union countries, this would add to the stimulus because Europe is an important source of investment for the LAC region and a significant market for the region's exports, especially for the countries in the Southern Cone of South America.

LAC relations with the United States are by no means optimal at the moment. Since the terrorist attack of September 11, 2001, the United States has largely ignored Latin America and the Caribbean and has given security a higher priority than economic relations with the region. There have been differences, as well, over U.S. policy in Iraq. Two LAC countries then on the United Nations Security Council, Mexico and Chile, indicated they would not support the U.S.-sponsored second resolution on Iraq, and this aroused considerable petulance in the U.S. government. Having said this, economic growth in the United States, which undoubtedly would help stimulate economic growth in the LAC, would temporarily trump the region's current inchoate hostility toward the United States. The most important gift that the United States can give to LAC is to grow faster.

13 THE DOLLARIZATION DEBATE*

Popular and professional distrust of the durability of established exchange rates contributed to practically all the financial collapses of recent years, from Mexico in 1994–1995 to Brazil in 1998–1999. Capital exited from the hapless nations—these two and others, such as Thailand, Indonesia, Russia, and Ecuador—in dramatic fashion, and the end result was a depreciation of the currency accompanied by collapses in real activity (production, sales, salaries, and other income). The extensive human hardships dominated discussion within the affected countries, such as in Ecuador now, whereas the technical financial aspects received the bulk of international media attention at the time the events were unfolding.

Exchange-rate arrangements have been a constant theme for centuries, indeed millennia, ever since countries with different currencies began trading with each other. Many arrangements endured over long periods, only to collapse when faced with unacceptable strains. One rule that most economists now accept is that there is no single exchange-rate arrangement that is optimal for all countries—or for individual countries—at all times. The gold standard gave way in the 1920s and 1930s, the adjustable peg structure of the International Monetary Fund in the early 1970s, and more recently so did a crawling peg set in a band around a dominant currency, such as the dollar.

The current wisdom is that only two systems, which on the surface are diametrically opposed, can endure for extended periods in the modern world of growing international trade, investment, and capital movements. These are *rigid exchange rates*, of which dollarization is one form, and *freely floating rates*, which permit the currency to roll with shocks without sacrifice of foreign reserves in a way that adjustable or crawling pegs cannot. Mexico and Brazil, while their financial crises played out, had currencies pegged to the dollar in a narrow band that they protected by selling reserves (buying their own currencies) to keep their currencies from depreciating outside the band. In each case, after losing tens of billions of dollars of reserves, they gave up the battle and

---

* *Issues in International Political Economy*, no. 2 (February 2000).

floated their currencies. So did Chile, more recently, as a prudent measure. In each case the float is working well—at least so far. The currencies are fluctuating, but not inordinately so, and all three economies are performing well. These are really the first serious experiments with floating rates in major economies of Latin America.

Argentina has a rigid system under which the peso is convertible with the dollar, on demand, at a 1:1 ratio. This system was introduced as a way to eliminate Argentina's habitual inflation and it has accomplished this. The Argentine system removed the monetary policy authority of the central bank and set up a requirement that dollar holdings must equal the full extent of the country's monetary base (the currency in circulation plus the reserves of the banking system).

The system is not foolproof. Argentina had to scramble to line up contingent dollar backing, which it did successfully, after the tequila effect of the Mexican devaluation in 1994. Argentina was hit much harder after Brazil devalued its currency in 1999 because the peso became sharply overvalued in relation to the Brazilian real. About a third of Argentina's exports go to Brazil, and the Brazilian financial-economic crisis had more severe effects on Argentina than on Brazil itself. The then-president of Argentina, Carlos Menem, suggested that Argentina should become even more rigid in its currency valuation and shift from a currency board to full dollarization. He argued just this month that all the countries in the Americas should adopt the dollar to avoid devaluations. When the Ecuadorian economy collapsed this year, its president, Jamil Mahuad, proposed that Ecuador should dollarize.

What is meant by dollarization? What are its attractions? Why is dollarization resisted, both popularly (the suggestion of Ecuador's president to do this contributed to his ouster) and technically? The crisis in Mercosur this past year was the consequence of incompatible exchange-rate arrangements between the two important trading partners, Brazil and Argentina. Are there options to deal with this inconsistency other than dollarization? Should the United States react to other countries adopting its currency as their official money? So far the U.S. government has been cool to the idea.

The dollar is used for many purposes: it is the most important currency in international trade transactions; dollars are held as foreign reserves more than any other currency; individuals and companies fearful about the stability of their own currency hold dollars to safeguard the real value of their assets. Many contracts in foreign countries—such as leases—are expressed in dollars to protect against national inflation and effective depreciation of the national currency. The argument often made is that many countries—Mexico is an example—are already de facto dollarized and why not take the next step and dollarize de jure.

There is an important difference between official and haphazard dollarization. Under official dollarization, the internal debt of governments and individuals is in dollars, accounting practices will have to change, and dollars cease to be foreign reserves and instead become the national currency. The process of transformation is complex; for example, an exchange rate must be chosen to convert existing contracts, assets, debts, and the like into dollars. The sharp depreciation of the Ecuadorian sucre to a level of 25,000 per dollar has made many Ecuadorians nervous about their president's proposal to dollarize.

Dollarization has both an upside and a downside for foreign countries. The main advantage is that it can give confidence that the value of the currency will be stable, at least more so than most national currencies. Many traders see this as critical. This was evident in Mexico, which experienced sharp currency devaluations roughly every six years from 1976 to 1994, corresponding with national presidential elections. The fear that this will happen again in 2000, an election year, guided much economic policy of the current administration. The past devaluations took place when Mexico tried to protect the value of the peso vis-à-vis the dollar within a narrow band whereas the Mexican peso is now floating more or less freely.

One downside is that the country loses seigniorage, which is essentially the interest lost on foreign reserves held in dollars. The seigniorage loss can be hundreds of millions of dollars a year, depending on the extent of the reserves. A more serious issue is that a balance-of-payments disequilibrium, such as a large current account deficit, cannot be corrected by a depreciation of the currency—the national currency no longer exists—but must instead be corrected by a contraction of the domestic economy. It was the unwillingness to accept this outcome that eventually did in the gold standard.

Dollarization means that a country gives up an independent monetary policy and relies instead on the policy of the Federal Reserve Board of the United States. This entails a clear loss of economic sovereignty. Many analysts consider this an advantage in that central banks in many developing countries do not have stellar records of promoting monetary stability. They are often under the political control of governments and are ordered to "print" money to finance government deficits, and this will not be possible if dollarization is to succeed.

Indeed, dollarization will not succeed unless fiscal policy is highly disciplined. Financing public sector deficits means taking on dollar debt and there is a limit to the extent this can be done. Many advocates of dollarization also see this as an advantage because it can impose the discipline that might not otherwise exist. Panama, which has been dollarized since early in the twentieth century, has shown that fiscal self-restraint is feasible.

Dollarization does not mean absolute stability of the currency in international markets. The dollar itself floats and there have been wide changes in the relationships among the three major world currencies, the dollar, euro, and yen. If the dollar depreciates (appreciates) with respect to either of the other two currencies, this will affect the trade of a dollarized country. There is reasonable certainty of the value of the dollar, but not absolute certainty.

The European Union chose to move to a single currency, the euro, to avoid sharp changes in the values of the separate currencies and to reduce transaction costs of changing from one currency to another. There has been talk of potential monetary union (dollarization) in North America—among Canada, Mexico, and the United States, the three members of NAFTA—for the same reason. None of the three countries now supports this, but the idea is in the public domain. Many analysts believe that Mercosur, the common market of south—composed of Argentina, Brazil, Paraguay, and Uruguay—should move toward a monetary union of its own, but Brazil does not support this and the position of the other three countries is uncertain.

One question often asked is whether a dollarized Western Hemisphere is inevitable on the grounds that its economic advantages outweigh the political and symbolic sovereignty disadvantages. The European Union came this conclusion, even though many countries still do not accept this—the United Kingdom, for one, at least for now. Few things other than death merit the descriptor "inevitable." What is clear, however, is that the issue of dollarization is now on the agenda and is unlikely to disappear.

14 THE ROLE OF THE LEADING INTERNATIONAL ECONOMIC ORGANIZATIONS*

The salient issue regarding the future of the World Trade Organization, the International Monetary Fund, and the World Bank is not whether organized street demonstrations can disrupt their meetings. Nor is it the inability of the more than 130 member countries in each of them to reach agreement at any particular meeting on the complex and politically sensitive issues they must confront. It is, rather, whether each of them still performs the valuable function of facilitating global economic growth, development, and stability in ways that other institutions, or the unfettered workings of the market, cannot.

This does not mean that these organizations should be immune from constructive criticism or that they can operate without taking into account the nature of the times. Much recent criticism, however, cites particular failures of the institutions—such as a number of questionable environmental decisions by the World Bank and the underestimation by the IMF of the extent of the economic fallout in East Asia when the financial crisis erupted in Thailand in 1997—merely to advocate their complete elimination. There is considerable trashing of the three institutions by ideologues from both the left and the right. It is no secret that the Heritage Foundation and the *Wall Street Journal* will mercilessly attack the IMF and the World Bank at every opportunity, and that Pat Buchanan, Ralph Nader, and the AFL-CIO can be counted on to castigate the efforts of the WTO to facilitate open trade. Such ideologues are rarely receptive to information that contradicts their preconceptions.

The WTO (and the General Agreement on Tariffs and Trade before it) was created to reduce the trade barriers that were so destructive of international economic development in the years between the two world wars. The GATT was remarkably successful in this task, so much so that tariffs of developed countries have largely ceased to be impediments to trade, and quantitative restrictions on industrial products are the exception and not the norm. As border barriers diminished, the GATT turned to other tasks, such as internal measures designed to impede the

---

* *Issues in International Political Economy*, no. 5 (May 2000).

flow of goods, such as marketing structures within countries, and liberalizing trade in information, financial, and other services. The dispute-settlement system in the GATT was flawed in that the country against which a complaint was lodged could effectively block efforts to examine the issue. The revised dispute-settlement system in the WTO was pushed by the United States to overcome this problem. Criticism from those who argue that the United States sacrifices its sovereignty when it loses arbitration decisions deliberately ignores the fact that the United States, which wins more cases than it loses, cannot win all of them in the WTO's quasi-judicial conflict resolution structure.

Perhaps the major function of the World Trade Organization is to provide a forum for international discussion and then implementation of trade policy. If there were no WTO, a replacement body would have to be invented because international trade, by definition, involves many nations. The virtue of the WTO is that it provides a rules-based system rather than one under which all disputes are resolved by power contests. Do the critics of the WTO really want the United States to dictate to the rest of the world what the relationships should be between trade and the environment, or trade and labor? Would they really want trade disputes resolved by retaliation and counterretaliation, rather than discussion? Is trade war superior to trade jaw-jaw? I think not.

The International Monetary Fund is undergoing considerable change. Secrecy is giving way to transparency. Lawrence Summers, secretary of the U.S. Treasury, has suggested that the IMF focus on short-term crisis prevention and resolution and not seek to replace the private market for long-term provision of credit. Should the IMF also provide large-scale emergency assistance, conditioned by corrective action taken by the affected country, in those exceptional cases when a crisis might compromise the larger financial structure? This was the case in Mexico in 1995. This is an area where reasonable people can disagree. I think it should, whereas Allan Meltzer, the chairman of the Advisory Commission on International Financial Institutions, wrote at the time that it should not. Meltzer's concern was over moral hazard. He argued that the IMF and the U.S. Treasury were bailing out private investors (which they were), and that getting out of these crises should be left to the workings of the private market. Yes, the private market would eventually have resolved the problem—just as the Great Depression in the United States in the early 1930s would have been resolved without government intervention—but over a longer time frame and with more protracted suffering. Mexico returned to a solid growth path less than a year after the bailout and repaid its emergency debt to the United States, with interest, well in advance of the due date.

The current emphasis of the World Bank is on poverty reduction and away from infrastructure financing. In point of fact, the new emphasis omits the earlier rationale that poverty reduction is best achieved in an atmosphere of economic growth and that economic growth requires infrastructure, such as farm-to-market roads, good seaports and airports, irrigation, and water purification facilities. The World Bank president makes the indisputable point that development is a holistic endeavor that must involve education and healthcare as well as physical facilities.

Demonstrations to achieve change in public policies are a legitimate and traditional tool in the United States. The Million Mom March in Washington, D.C., on May 14, 2000, in favor of gun control is the latest example of this. Martin Luther King drew large and peaceful crowds seeking an end to racial division. These demonstrations were based on achieving specific objectives, whereas those in Seattle and Washington directed against the WTO, the IMF, and the World Bank were inchoate and intended more to demolish than to build. One positive objective of the demonstrations against the IMF and the World Bank was to advocate debt reduction for the poorest countries, an initiative the IMF already had taken.

There is clearly a philosophic divide in the country concerning the role of international economic institutions. The only common ground among the demonstrators that I could discern was distrust of large, transnational corporations. This led the disparate group to disparage the very institutions that foster international cooperation among governments. On the other side of this divide is the belief that there is an intergovernmental role for promoting trade, since without it the poor countries will never develop; that the international community should seek to prevent and mitigate financial crises when prevention fails rather than stand by regardless of the consequences; and that concessional loans and grants to developing countries are worthy endeavors. The details of how these tasks are accomplished must change over time and are not necessarily ideal at present, but U.S. destruction or withdrawal from these institutions would be a tragic error.

15 CRITICAL ASPECTS OF THE GLOBAL ECONOMY*

When the word "globalization" is uttered, it evokes two contradictory visceral reactions: it is either the essential element of recent U.S. competitiveness; or it is inherently evil because the global spread of multinational corporations enriches the wealthy and economically powerful at the expense of the vast multitude of workers. In what follows, I will avoid both attacks and praise, and instead focus on key features of international trade and investment that characterize what is taking place in much of the world.

A country, if its dictatorial leader so insists, can set its own prohibitive tariff and import structure and reject foreign investment. North Korea and Vietnam, both nondemocratic, did this for many years, despite the horrible cost this policy imposed on national welfare. This isolation is breaking down in these two countries, even as it did earlier in China after the death of Mao, and for much the same reason. Eternal poverty is not a good formula for regime continuity.

Guarding economic sovereignty did not take the same absolutist form in most other countries, but a profound transformation is taking place in them as well. Import barriers are coming down and attacks against foreign investment are being transmuted into searches to attract foreign investment. Mexico, before its debt collapse in 1982, favored external borrowing over investment to obtain foreign exchange, but learned to its dismay that this practice contained its own risks when the debt could not be serviced. The philosophic base of development then changed and foreign investment was actively sought as an essential requirement for Mexico to augment its exports. This outlook was the premise of NAFTA. Hugo Chávez, the president of Venezuela, rails against primitive neoliberalism *(neoliberalismo salvaje)*, but nevertheless has kept the country's import tariffs relatively low, even as he makes a great effort to obtain foreign direct investment to develop his country's telecommunications and natural gas activities. Chávez, so far, has shown a tendency to talk like a Marxist, much like Fidel Castro, his romantic icon, but then act like a capitalist.

For many of the world's poorest countries, the primordial problem is not the spread of multinational corporations, but their inability to

---

* *Issues in International Political Economy*, no. 11 (November 2000).

participate in the process. This is especially true in sub-Saharan Africa. Their poverty, small internal markets, and accompanying political instability make them poor destinations for foreign investment, other than to exploit minerals for export. This does not lead to substantial job creation.

Both foreign direct investment and international trade are growing more rapidly than world economic growth. This is a clear manifestation that the "foreign" aspect of the world economy is becoming increasingly important. If one looks back only 20 years, when the dominant economic model in Latin America was to develop behind high import barriers and to downplay the importance of exports, it is startling how much development thinking has changed in that part of the world. East Asia, with its export orientation, became the model, and not the preachings of those who advised Latin America to look inward.

The bulk of the world's trade is carried on by large corporations. This is not a new phenomenon. These same corporations are large investors in foreign manufacturing and service activities. Indeed, the two phenomena—investing and producing in foreign countries and then selling much of the output in still other foreign countries, as well as the home market—are inseparable.

International trade is increasingly taking place in intermediate rather than final products—chips for computers, parts for office machinery, engines for automobiles and trucks, cotton and wool fabrics for apparel. Look under the hood of your car; the transmission assembly may have elements produced in a number of countries. The assembly line in Detroit works on a just-in-time basis to receive the material needed from across the border in Windsor, Ontario—and beware of a slowdown from a customs snafu that leads to a costly disruption in the manufacturing process.

This goes by the name "coproduction." The parts are produced in a variety of locations, assembled in other places, and sold globally. Much of the sales are within the same multinational corporation, say, from a parent to a subsidiary (intra-firm trade), or within the same sector (intra-industry trade). As goods pass across borders in this fashion, the absence of border impediments (tariffs, lengthy inspection delays) is crucial, as the automotive example between Windsor and Detroit exemplifies. Hence, the drive for trade negotiations to lower these barriers and the proliferation of regional economic integration agreements, such as NAFTA, to legally ensure the absence of delays in a just-in-time world.

Economic integration, and, by extension, the process of globalization, is centered on competition in particular sectors when it comes to production and merchandise trade. What is taking place is a form of division of labor—Adam Smith on a regional and global scale. The global aspect is made possible by technology, advances in communication and transportation, and by financing far more vast than anything seen before. Corporations take many factors into account when setting up complementary plants in foreign countries, such as size of the domestic market, the availability and price of labor, the cost of transportation, and the political stability of the country where the investment is made. The growth of U.S. coproduction with Mexico was based primarily on two considerations: proximity, and thus low transportation costs; and inexpensive labor. Most foreign direct investment is made among industrial countries, which is evidence that cheap labor is by no means always the dominant criterion. This is evident as well from the paucity of investment in the world's poorest countries.

If most international trade is conducted by large corporations, what does this imply for the future of small- and medium-sized enterprises? In just about all countries, goods and services that are not internationally traded are more voluminous than tradables. In addition, many large corporations have concluded that making all inputs in-house is not the most efficient practice and instead are subcontracting to independent producers and service providers—and many of these are relatively small enterprises. Their products are then exported indirectly, via the exports of the large corporations.

There is no intent in this discussion to assert that multinational corporations invariably provide their workers with optimal working conditions and good salaries and are always careful to avoid environmental degradation in their operations. We know that many corporations are not that meticulous, even though we also know that wages and working conditions in foreign transplants generally are superior to those of domestic enterprises. We know that foreign trade and investment results in losers in the home countries, although by now it is clear that there are many more winners. We know that the global spread of business benefits some countries more than others and that some regions of countries prosper while others lag behind. The globalization genie—in the form of investment, trade, financial flows, and technology advances—is out of the bottle. The challenges are to minimize the downside dangers while exploiting the upside benefits that globalization can offer to countries throughout the world.

16 SOME HIGHLIGHTS IN THE GLOBAL ECONOMY IN 2000*

This is the last commentary of the first year of monthly musings on issues in international political economy, and the end of a year is a good time to strike some kind of balance. What follow are thoughts on the year's political economy highlights, some somber and others encouraging.

THE DISCOURAGING DEVELOPMENTS

1. *Not only has there been limited progress in global trade negotiations, but there has been a heightening of trade conflict, especially between the United States and the European Union.* Each side has been pushing hard to show its toughness, almost like children trying to outdo each other. I will give just two examples, the U.S. action on bananas and the EU's attack on the U.S. use of foreign sales corporations, or FSCs, to promote exports.

Each side, based on the letter of the law as expressed in the World Trade Organization (and its predecessor, the General Agreement on Tariffs and Trade), won cases against the other that held up on appeal. Each measure—the way the EU fashioned its banana preferences for ex-colonies and the tax benefit granted to U.S. multinational corporations—was bad policy. But the stridency of the retaliation was even worse. After winning its case, the United States proceeded to impose prohibitive tariffs on 42 kinds of products, all unrelated to bananas, whose imports from the EU amounted to $191.4 million. Lobbyists for some of the more important U.S. importers got the products they buy from the EU removed from the hit list, but many small U.S. importers did not even know enough to lobby. As far as the U.S. government was concerned, the system worked. EU discrimination against a product produced outside the United States but by a company (Chiquita Bananas) owned and managed by U.S. interests was punished. A principle was upheld: Thou shalt not discriminate. Another, more practical principle emerged: an influential person (the head of Chiquita Bananas) willing to use money to influence the political process can incite trade conflict.

* *Issues in International Political Economy*, no. 12 (December 2000).

The EU, after it won its complaint that the tax benefit provided to FSCs (corporations set up outside the United States through which domestic corporations channel exports of U.S. goods) was a subsidy, then sought to get WTO approval to retaliate against the United States. The EU assertion was that it should be allowed to raise prohibitive barriers against more than $4 billion (billion, with a "b") in imports from the United States unless the subsidy was eliminated. It is not clear whether this is a negotiating ploy or a firm intention.

FSCs have been in existence since 1984. Why did the EU wait until now to push its case? Was it retaliation for the banana case? The economics of the EU argument—as distinct from the legal provisions—are weak because subsidies of this type on the export of goods are largely neutralized by exchange-rate adjustments. Indeed, this was part of the European economic analysis when U.S. corporations argued years earlier that the EU use of value-added taxes, which are exempted when goods are exported, are unfair because U.S. income taxes are not similarly exempted when goods are sold abroad. In any event, here we are at war over subsidiary economic issues, when instead the dialogue between the world's two major exporters should be on making further progress in the reduction of a host of substantial barriers that affect trade.

2. Raucous demonstrations against the WTO, the World Bank, and the International Monetary Fund have become part of the background scenery of their meetings. Legitimate grievances (such as inadequate transparency of the proceedings of these organizations) are drowned out by a variety of other objectives, such as promoting anarchy, keeping delegates from getting to the sessions, destroying property to make a statement against multinational corporations, and preventing these global organizations from getting on with their assigned mandates. The target seems to be globalism, which is defined in whatever monstrous way the demonstrators see fit.

There is a legitimate case for peaceful public demonstrations, whether the argument being made is legitimate or not. The troubling aspect of the demonstrations being discussed is the ingathering for the purpose of shutting off speech through destructive means against organizations whose objectives represent the collective will of the international community. Developing countries will not benefit if they are unable to negotiate downward the barriers against their exports of goods and services, or if the World Bank has fewer resources to provide to them, or if the IMF cannot try to rescue these countries when their economies are in extremis.

3. *The final discouraging development of the year, that I will cite is the decline of democracy in Latin America.* U.S. administrations, from Reagan to Clinton, have repeated endlessly that all governments in the Western Hemisphere, except for Cuba, are democracies. This overstates, drastically so. We know that Haiti surely is not. Many Latin American countries have authoritarian systems, or venal leaders ("corruptocracies"), or survive based on the sufferance of military leaders. Governments of the Andean region are going through turmoil that makes it hard to define them as functioning democracies. Colombia is in the throes of civil and narcotics wars, Venezuela has no effective opposition to the current regime, Ecuador has been forced to change presidents because of conflict between the government on one side and military and indigenous groups on the other, Bolivia is finding it hard to make political decisions, and Peru's president found it necessary to resign, while in Japan, because of undoubted corruption.

There are some saving counterpoints. One is that the countries of the south—Brazil, Argentina, Chile, Uruguay—all dominated by the military during the 1980s—have become democratic once again and are now places where there is alternation of power between political parties. A second is that even the countries where democracies are fragile find it necessary to mouth democratic principles and at least show a façade of democracy. But the fact remains that there was severe democratic retrogression in Latin America this past year.

SOME ENCOURAGING DEVELOPMENTS

1. *Still on the democracy theme, the nonviolent transition of power in Mexico from the Institutional Revolutionary Party (PRI) to Vicente Fox, the candidate of the conservative National Action Party (but representing a more diverse coalition—those supporting any credible candidate not from the PRI), was a signal accomplishment.* The PRI had controlled the presidency for 71 years until Fox was inaugurated on December 1, 2000. Different analysts have their own explanations for why the change took place, including Fox's charisma, the colorless PRI presidential candidate, public impatience after 71 years of one-party rule, the stress on

market economics during the past 15 years, the repeated financial crises every six years since the mid-1970s, the painful economic downturn in 1995 after an unsuccessful currency devaluation in December 1994, the slow opening of the political system after the 1968 student demonstrations, and others.

No one can predict how successful President Fox's economic, social, and anticorruption policies will be. However, the peaceful transference of power after a generally honest election in the second-largest country in Latin America was itself a big event. Forty or more heads of state attended the inaugural. The pity was the absence of Bill Clinton, the president of Mexico's most important partner and neighbor country.

2. Also, in contrast to the senseless demonstrations noted above, the heads of developing countries generally aspired to live with and take advantage of the globalization taking place in economics, finance, communication, and technology. Most developing country leaders who spoke up during the year wanted to join the world, not stop it. I saved this point for the end because it may be the most hopeful development in international political economy during 2000.

17 IDEOLOGICAL GENERALIZATIONS ABOUT FINANCIAL RESCUE PACKAGES*

Financial rescues sometimes work and frequently fail. The Mexico rescue in 1995 accomplished everything that was expected of it whereas the Russian rescue in 1998 did not. There are ideologues, however, who curse any rescue—even when it works. When Treasury secretary Paul O'Neill said at his confirmation hearing that he hoped he would be given the freedom to do what seemed necessary when his Mexico occurred, the *Wall Street Journal*, in an editorial on January 24, called this a "beleaguered" view.

My purpose in what follows is to be practical and not partisan or dogmatic. Allan Meltzer, who is a respected professor at Carnegie Mellon University, has become something of a guru for those who oppose rescues under any circumstances. This prominence is based on a report in March 2000 of the International Financial Advisory Commission, which he chaired. There was a flat statement in that report that "the Mexican program established several bad precedents." The basis for this statement was that the Clinton administration ignored congressional opposition to the expenditure of funds for the rescue, and instead went ahead with credits of up to $20 billion from the Exchange Stabilization Fund.

The philosophic opposition to the Mexico package, and by extension to other sizeable financial rescues, rests on two facets of what, in the financial world, is referred to as "moral hazard." Moral hazard, in essence, means that individuals or countries accept financial risks they would not otherwise take only because they know or expect they will be bailed out if things go wrong. The Federal Deposit Insurance Company insures individual bank deposits of up to $100,000 against risks. The U.S. government bailed out the Chrysler Corporation. Moral hazard enters into these actions, just as it does when there is a sense that some banks or financial institutions are too large to fail. The moral hazard argument against financial rescues is that countries ignore prudent economic policies if they can count on being rescued. Individual investors, the argument goes, downplay the risks they are taking when they seek high returns because they expect to be bailed out.

---

* *Issues in International Political Economy*, no. 15 (March 2001).

This reasoning is pervasive in the Meltzer commission report. Is it valid? Does the need to avoid moral hazard override all other considerations when the International Monetary Fund, or the U.S. government, supports country rescue packages? I will take up these questions in turn, particularly as they refer to the Mexican rescue. (In the interest of full disclosure, I dealt with the Mexican case in detail in a book entitled *Financial Decision-Making in Mexico.*[1])

In the Mexican case, many individuals held government debt instruments called *tesobonos* that were short-term peso obligations indexed to the dollar—in effect, dollar obligations—that earned a higher interest rate than could be obtained by investing in U.S. government notes or bonds. The holders of tesobonos—individuals, pension funds, and Mexicans and foreigners alike—were paid off to the tune of $20 billion-plus that was outstanding at the end of 1994. This was moral hazard and highly unfortunate. Risk takers pocket the benefits of the chances they take and they should be expected to bear the costs when the investment sours. The problem was that there was no straightforward way for Mexico to meet its obligations and not make whole the holders of tesobonos. The conclusion reached was that accepting this form of moral hazard was less costly to the Mexican population than foregoing the entire rescue package.

The moral hazard question becomes even dicier when it applies to a whole country. The Mexican economic authorities took what I think were unforgivable risks. That is why I subtitled my book "To Bet a Nation." But to jump from this conclusion to the assertion that they took those risks because they expected to be made whole defies logic. Despite the rescue, Mexican gross domestic product plunged in 1995 by some 7 percent, consumption and investment together fell by 16 percent, inflation jumped to 52 percent, real wages dropped by almost 20 percent, unemployment increased by about 1 million, and the peso fell by more than 43 percent over the course of the year. Yes, there was a rescue package, but the cost to the Mexican people was staggering. Those who argue that moral hazard makes recklessness cost-free surely cannot include the Mexican case in their reasoning.

My explanation for the behavior of Mexican policymakers in 1994 focuses on politics and on habits of decisionmaking built up over many years. Devaluation of the overvalued peso was ruled out in advance of the presidential election in August 1994. A disproportionate bet was made after August that the devaluation could be delayed until early in

1995, when a new administration was in power. Long-entrenched habits of secrecy led to the exclusion from policy meetings of people who disagreed with the financial policies being followed. It was reprehensible to delay the deluge until somebody else's presidential watch, but this is not moral hazard in the meaning ascribed to this phrase by the ideological opposition to financial rescues.

One other aspect of the philosophic mind-set of those who oppose any official rescue efforts is that the market should be allowed to correct policy mistakes: "The market is sacred—do not interfere with it." The market undoubtedly will correct errors, taking its time as it does. Mexico regained access to international financial lending within five months of the December 1994 collapse, or less than four months after the rescue. It took almost seven years for Mexico to regain such access after the country's 1982 debt crisis, which was not dealt with decisively by external creditors. Mexico has had solid GDP growth year in and year out since 1996—indeed, Mexico is one of Latin America's leading economic performers these past five years. George Shultz is cited frequently for his 1998 statement, "As is typical when the IMF intervenes, the governments and the lenders were rescued, but not the people." Mr. Shultz is half-right in the Mexican case—the lenders were rescued, but the Mexican people surely would be worse off today if they were left to stew in the mess created by their departing leaders in 1994.

The Mexican rescue took place because the U.S. authorities then in place—President Clinton, Treasury Secretary Robert Rubin, Deputy Treasury Secretary Larry Summers, and Federal Reserve Chairman Alan Greenspan—were prepared to look at the potential consequences of a non-rescue. Rightly or wrongly, they feared a fallout on the U.S. financial structure if the Mexican situation was allowed to fester as the market worked out its correction over many years. The rescue worked and all U.S. credits were repaid, at premium interest rates. Mexico today has investor-grade ratings in international money markets. The country achieved solid economic growth once the corrective measures required under the rescue were put in place. Perhaps most important, Mexico today has a political structure far more democratic than that which existed before.

Mexico, however, is not a good template for other potential rescues by the United States. For one, Mexico is next door. The United States has a free-trade agreement with Mexico and trade between the two countries is booming. There is no way to keep instability in Mexico in a lockbox to prevent contamination to the United States—to U.S. financial, commercial, labor, and other markets. The economies and cultures of the two countries are much too intertwined for U.S. authorities to take the position of "let Mexico be damned" if leaders take unwise or unwarranted actions. Beyond this, the Mexican authorities were prepared to take corrective economic measures, which has not always been true in other instances of potential rescue.

This leads me to the pragmatic conclusion that our new treasury secretary should be given what he said he wanted—namely, discretion to act in the way he thinks correct when his Mexico financial crisis arises.

Note

[1] Sidney Weintraub, *Financial Decision-Making in Mexico: To Bet a Nation* (Pittsburgh, Pa.: University of Pittsburgh Press, 2000).

18 THE TERRORIST ATTACK: TREATING THE CAUSES[*]

We have been hearing much since September 11 that the United States, to avoid future terrorist attacks, must treat the causes. Which causes? Should the treatment deal with reversing the terrorists' hatred for the United States, eliminating anti-Jewish sentiment, correcting the lack of freedom in most Middle Eastern countries, refighting the Kosovo war and getting some Americans killed, making too many or too few charges against foreign human rights violations, eliminating homosexuality and civil liberties in the United States (as Jerry Falwell and Pat Robertson seem to believe), altering the capitalist system that prevails in the developed countries, changing the U.S. lifestyles that so infuriate Muslim zealots, reducing poverty?

No shortage of "causes"—some outrageous, others idiosyncratic, and some even with a sense of legitimacy—have been put forward that should be treated. The monthly commentaries in this issues series deal with political economy and I will stick (mostly) to the last and focus on poverty. However, this must be prefaced with a caveat. I find it impossible that anyone can seriously believe that because there is much poverty in the Middle East, terrorists who are not themselves poor concluded that the corrective was to attack the World Trade Center towers and the Pentagon and kill thousands of innocent people.

I am focusing on poverty because it is a global scourge and we would have a better world if poverty could be reduced drastically. One consequence of the events on September 11 will be to sharply increase poverty because of the ripple effects on developing countries from the economic troubles of the United States and other industrial countries. Markets for the goods and services of developing countries will shrink, as will investment in them. When the economies of rich countries decline, the suffering from the fallout is usually greater in poor countries. This, for better or worse, is part of globalism.

Many implicitly assume that the reduction of poverty has been neglected up until now. This is not true. What is correct, however, is that the world has not been overwhelmingly effective in dealing with the problem. The number of people who live below the poverty line is now

---

[*] *Issues in International Political Economy*, no. 22 (October 2001).

about 1.3 billion. This is an enormous figure, even though the proportion of the world's population living in poverty has declined more in the past 50 years than in the previous 500 years. The absolute number, however, has risen.

Poverty is not an independent manifestation isolated from development strategies and politics within countries, but part and parcel of the bigger picture. I have not understood the motivations of the protesters who show up to disrupt meetings of international development and trade organizations because precisely these institutions have taken the lead to reduce poverty. Poverty did not begin with globalization. The proportion of people living in poverty has not increased because globalization has made communications and financial transfers more efficient than ever before. If anything, globalization is an opportunity to reduce levels of poverty because linkages between developed and developing countries are now so intense.

Poverty reduction clearly goes hand-in-hand with economic growth. Overall economic growth is insufficient to reduce poverty, but it is the essential ingredient. Redistribution without growth merely rearranges the scenery, but does not get at the core of the problem. Poverty-reduction policy, therefore, must be an ingredient of development policy. And that is the rub: no simple, sure-fire formula exists for converting a stagnant, low-income country into a vibrant one with a growing economy.

Development is a slow, slogging, arduous process that must deal with big-picture matters, such as macroeconomic policy and microeconomic issues of industrial and agricultural development and the building of solid institutions. Education must be a priority, and this cannot be accomplished in one decade or one generation. Infant mortality is higher and life expectancy is lower in developing countries because of inadequate health care. Countries need roads to bring goods to market, equity in land tenure, ports, an adequate and safe water supply, and the infrastructure that makes development possible. Poverty reduction, if all of these needs are met, must then be a conscious part of government programs, which is why bumper-sticker slogans like "Reduce Poverty" are fatuous. By all means, let us work to reduce poverty, but the issue must be treated more seriously than a politician's or an editorialist's spin might suggest.

The history of today's developed countries, as widely documented, is that poverty actually increased during the early years of the development process. Investments during the early days of the growth process tended to direct resources to immediately productive activities and only after the cumulative effects of these development accomplishments reached a pivotal point did poverty and inequality decline. Thus one may make a case for directing more resources to developing countries, but they must be part of a viable development program. And, yes, the United States has not in recent years been a generous aid donor in relation to the U.S. gross domestic product. Politicians say that foreign aid is not popular because it helps foreigners. Yes, it does, but what is wrong with that?

The discussion of poverty reduction can be brought specifically to the situation in the Middle East and South Asia. Most people in those regions, which seem to be the cradle of the terrorism movement, live in poverty. Not a single country in the Middle East, save Israel, has a democratic government. Population growth rates are high and this adds to the costs of development. Yet, the priorities of dictatorial leaders, whether religious or otherwise, are not economics—or reducing poverty—but a host of other issues, from religious fanaticism to political dominance to a hatred of neighbors.

Is this situation mainly the fault of the United States? Does the existence of Israel impoverish its Arab enemies? The answer to both questions is, of course, no. Has the United States made errors in the ways it has interacted with countries in the Middle East? Has Israel? Yes, both countries have. But to then leap from this to the assertion that the attacks were justified, that the United States got what it deserved, is insane. Has the United States provided benefits and favors to countries in the Middle East? The answer is surely yes, more so than any other country.

Countries make their own development policies. Unless a country makes a development policy its own, the reality that aid will accomplish little has long been a truism among development-assistance practitioners. Donor countries and agencies can give advice and provide technical and financial resources, but they cannot impose programs that national leaders do not want, a lesson that has been learned repeatedly. Aid donors cannot eliminate corruption; leaders of countries must do that. The donors cannot insist that dictatorial regimes be transformed into democracies; they can withhold aid or they can grant it and hope that some start at development will lead to more satisfactory regimes. If economic development and the installation of democracy are unimportant in the agendas of foreign leaders, neither the United States nor other donors have much power to alter the situation.

To return to where this commentary began, poverty is a deep-seated plague, one that the world must deal with on moral and practical grounds. It is impossible to will away poverty; getting rid of poverty takes consistent dedication. Poverty has been reduced sharply in some countries because their leaders and priorities of governance sincerely sought economic growth and poverty reduction. The number of poor has been reduced as a proportion of world population because of the economic system put into effect after World War II. However, the job is far from accomplished and deserves a sustained effort to do better in the future.

19 REVIVING THE U.S. ECONOMY*

My impression of the post–September 11 economic maneuverings of the administration and of its allies in the House of Representatives is that they saw and seized a double opportunity to promote their ideology. The first objective was to reward business with tax favors, over and above those enacted in the tax legislation earlier this year—whether or not these favors provide short-term economic stimulus. The second goal was to continue to starve the federal government of resources in order to keep key activities, such as airport security, in private hands—despite the manifest shortcomings of this security prior to September 11.

Lobbyists pushing for favors, from tax breaks to import protection for their business clients, have swamped the halls of Congress. This was evident in the fight to prevent making airport security personnel federal employees. The airline industry was given funds immediately. The insurance industry comes next. Steel protection is likely to be augmented. The Senate Finance Committee, controlled by the Democrats, included special tax breaks in its version of an economic stimulus bill for citrus growers, crop dusters, and other agricultural interests. I am a big enough boy and therefore expect self-interest to manifest itself even in a time of crisis, but I had hoped that the federal government—and the Congress—would have loftier goals. In a moment of candor, Paul O'Neill, the secretary of the treasury, labeled the party-line vote on the House Ways and Means Committee economic stimulus package as "show business"—of the members showing their benefactors which side they are on.

The media have focused much attention on the provision in the House "stimulus" bill to repeal the corporate alternative minimum tax retroactively to 1986, which would provide a windfall of about $25 billion to some of the United States' largest corporations. This provision may not survive the House-Senate reconciliation that is sure to come, but that this handout was included at all in the name of stimulus is distressing. At the same time, the bill provided stingy resources for augmented unemployment compensation or help in maintaining health insurance at a time when hundreds of thousands of workers are losing jobs.

---

* *Issues in International Political Economy*, no. 23 (November 2001).

I do not wish to berate the Republicans alone. It is mostly the Democrats in the Congress who are fighting to prevent negotiations to lower trade barriers, even though we have long known that open trade raises global welfare. A recent World Bank analysis concluded that developing countries stand to gain about $1.5 trillion of additional income in the 10 years after trade liberalization is begun and that developed countries would see their income rise by $1.3 trillion. Import protectionism at a time of a declining economy was the tragic formula at the onset of the great depression of the 1930s. Today's protectionism is not of the same order, but it is there—and especially against goods exported by poor countries, mainly textile and agricultural products.

The U.S. economy does need stimulation. The Federal Reserve Board is doing what it can by lowering interest rates, but we do not know how effective this has been or will be. What is at issue is the nature of the fiscal program to augment the monetary stimulus. This can be done in a number of ways, such as increasing government spending or lowering tax receipts. John Maynard Keynes, whom supply-siders vilified for many years, is suddenly much in fashion. However, those who seek to reduce taxes for a decade or more into the future are misinforming the public about Keynesianism. Keynes did not advocate perpetual fiscal deficits, but rather to vary fiscal policy in a countercyclical way— to have deficits in bad times to increase demand, and thereby stimulate economic activity, and surpluses in good times to moderate inflation.

Keynesian thinking fell out of favor largely because the U.S. legislative process is so lengthy that by the time a fiscal stimulus could be put into effect, the economy recovered on its own and the stimulus would thus have a perverse effect. This time, however, it seemed possible to take the necessary stimulative measures in real time before the economy reached bottom. To take this thinking one step further, this implies that the resources should be injected quickly to augment demand and then removed when no longer needed.

Quickly disbursing government expenditures can accomplish this, as President George W. Bush recognized when he sent envelopes with $300 or $600 in cash earlier this year to those who paid income taxes. The idea was that this windfall would be spent, and we now know that this was not necessarily the case for middle- and higher-income taxpayers. Checks could be sent this time to those who earn too little to pay any or much income tax and thereby have more assurance that the funds will be spent. Payroll taxes could be forgiven for a reasonable time, thereby putting more money into the hands of probable spenders. The rationale of each of these techniques is to bolster consumption, which was a central element stimulating economic growth during the past several years, at least until this year. Each of these techniques has the virtue of directing funds to those who most need this support and of being self-limiting in time.

There have been arguments in favor of increased government spending to improve U.S. infrastructure, such as the inadequate rail system or urban transportation facilities in order to reduce automobile use and thereby conserve energy, or school buildings to replace those that are clearly inadequate. The problem here is that these are not short-term expenditures, nor are public construction projects quick disbursing. These are permanent needs and, if they make sense, should be included in ongoing budgets.

The stimulus legislation that passed in the House put most of its stress on tax incentives to encourage private investment. As with building needed infrastructure, encouraging investment over the long term is a proper function of growth policy. President John F. Kennedy's investment tax credit demonstrated this clearly in the 1960s. However, the current situation calls for a quick injection of funds to augment domestic demand. The longer-term, continuing needs should not be neglected, but they can be debated in their own right and not under the camouflage of emergency measures. In order for investment incentives to work in the short term, we must assume that companies are looking for incentives to invest. The evidence is just the reverse, namely, that there is considerable excess productive capacity.

The issues I raise here relate to the role and actions of a great power. The U.S. response to the September 11 terrorist attacks has many elements. The first task was to build a coalition to fight the source of that attack, and also to seek allies to punish terrorists generally. The United States is showing the kind of leadership one would expect in the military field. Similarly, leadership is being shown in the worldwide effort to cut off financing for terrorist activity. The events of September 11 also made abundantly clear that the United States was utterly unprepared to deal with the aftermath of the destruction in the homeland, or to safeguard against future terrorism that could be even more devastating than destroying buildings. The government and population of the United States, with some fits and starts and considerable uncertainty, are responding to all these imperatives.

However, the United States thus far is not showing the same leadership in the economic field. If the U.S. economy is slow to recover, as is likely if the stimulus is long-term rather than immediate, so too will economic recovery be delayed in much of the rest of the world. In each of the key areas—military, money laundering, and economic stimulus—the United States has a leadership obligation both to its national well-being and to the well-being of our friends and allies. A slow recovery will lead to more domestic unemployment and this will weaken public resolve to stay the course for the other elements of the anti-terrorist effort. The longer it takes for solid growth to resume in the United States, the greater will be the hardship elsewhere in the world, particularly in the poor countries that look to the U.S. market for their export revenue. The economic dimension of the war on terrorism is not a sideshow, but a central element if the entire effort is to be successful.

20 THE PRIMACY OF POLICY*

The founding fathers of the United States declared independence because the government under which they were living was depriving them of life, liberty, and the pursuit of happiness. The events of September 11 reinforced our knowledge about modern governments that terrorize their populations far more thoroughly than did the British crown in 1776. Many of today's governments do not secure life, but instead threaten it. There are no democracies among the Arab countries of the Middle East and no free press; hence, there is little liberty. The Taliban quite evidently does not believe in the pursuit of happiness; nor do many other dictatorial or fanatical governments that differ from the Taliban mainly in degree.

Governments facilitate the pursuit of happiness by establishing policies under which the population has access to education, health care, an ever-improving standard of living, and some confidence that opportunities for attaining these objectives will be greater for their children than for them. No government is perfect in pursuing happiness for all, but a successful government must have this as its objective. Many governments do not try; they seem to believe in the pursuit of misery. Others try, but only partially, and fail. These failures have consequences, internally, of course, but globally as well. That is the main point of this essay, that all of us pay a price for policy failures in distant lands.

The Arab countries, for the most part, have given priority to political issues, such as the destruction of Israel and the maintenance in power of authoritarian and dictatorial regimes. The end result has been the failure to achieve sustained economic growth. The desire of small cliques to obtain and retain power in many countries in Africa has also resulted in poor economic performance. Latin American leaders, for many years, even as they pursued misguided economic policies, had a tendency to blame others for their poor economic performance. Introspection about homegrown mistakes, which should be a necessary component in shaping economic policy, was neglected in the process. The Taliban, because of its zealous religious strictures, could never have delivered economic progress to the majority of its population.

---

* *Issues in International Political Economy*, no. 24 (December 2001).

If governments wish to achieve economic growth, there is no substitute for policies that give priority to this outcome. This does not mean that wise policies will always lead to satisfactory growth rates, but rather that inattention to policies to foster development will lead to low growth. By "growth policies" I have in mind those that deal with the well-being of the majority. Growth will be hampered if official corruption becomes a way of life. Isolation from world commerce and culture is a surefire way to fail economically. North Korea is the best example of this.

These thoughts come to me as I ponder the goals of Osama bin Laden and those who support him. Their goal is destruction—of the United States, of cultures different from their own—which, if successful, provides nothing for their own people. Argentina is on the verge of economic collapse, which has been caused in part by the inability of its political system to reach consensus over many decades on the key elements of economic growth. Robert Mugabe is tearing Zimbabwe apart in the name of holding on to political power. The Indonesian leaders gave priority to self-enrichment so that, when the financial bubble burst, they had little ability to overcome the economic crisis.

By contrast, after Mao departed the scene, the Chinese leaders gave priority to economic growth and the accomplishments have been impressive. Mexico, under Ernesto Zedillo, gave policy priority to economics rather than partisan politics and the result was both high growth and greater democracy. Chile in recent years placed its emphasis on economic accomplishment and outpaced the rest of the hemisphere in its growth rate.

The argument being made here is about the importance of policy and not that economics is more important than politics. However, if the politics are about destruction or self-aggrandizement, then economic outcomes almost surely will be unsatisfactory. If economic policy is designed to benefit the few rather than the majority, the politics are unlikely to be durable.

These are not abstract musings for their own sake, but rather are intended to examine one of the reasons for the great turmoil that exists in the world today. There has been much discussion about the causes of terrorism in the world, particularly after the attacks of September 11. These are not easy to pinpoint because not all terrorists are created from the same cloth. Al Qaeda, for example, grew out of religious zealotry, Sendero Luminoso in Peru out of a sense of injustice, and the Tamil insurgency against the government of Sri Lanka out of the lack of self-determination.

However, there are some common threads among these and other cases. These are the inadequacy of economic opportunity for the population of the countries involved (Afghanistan and the Arab countries, especially Egypt and Saudi Arabia, with respect to Al Qaeda), the absence of democracy (of liberty in the U.S. historical sense), and oppression of the many by the few who control the country. Most terrorism, as Kofi Annan emphasized in his speech accepting the Nobel Peace Prize, is directed internally, but the causes are probably the same when directed at outsiders. His theme, as I understand it, is that outside indifference to these internal injustices in the name of respecting sovereignty can no longer be tolerated.

When the ambitions of a restless population for economic and political opportunity are frustrated, there is a tendency to lash out, sometimes against the oppressors at home or those seen as oppressors in foreign countries. There is no foreign country that makes as good a target as the United States, the most powerful country in the world economically and militarily. The anger is sometimes cloaked in terms of U.S. interference, sometimes as cultural incompatibility. There may be a legitimate grievance—such as U.S. support of oppressive dictators—or there may not be, only internal seething and the need to lash out at someone.

The world pays a heavy price when priorities of failed and unjust states boil over in the search for scapegoats. We are witnessing the results of this phenomenon in Afghanistan. The failure of Arab countries to emphasize either economic growth or democracy has brought a heavy toll in destruction. The struggle for personal power in many African countries has worldwide repercussions. No one explanation fits all cases of terrorism, which can be practiced even when economic opportunity and political choice are not neglected—as is evident in Northern Ireland and in the Basque region of Spain—but much of the horror the world is witnessing today stems from misguided priorities.

There is no easy way for outsiders to alter failed policies, but there are some things that can be done. Economic assistance can be withheld from countries that do not give priority to economic growth on the grounds that outside resources can serve no useful purpose. The U.S. government can speak out forcefully when democracy is suppressed, as now appears to be happening in Zimbabwe. It is evident that if the U.S.

government walks away from reconstruction in Afghanistan, the economic-political situation would revert to chaos. We should not fail to intervene in the future, presumably through the United Nations, to stop tribal slaughter, as we failed in Burundi. Kofi Annan's theme that the world community cannot stand by and tolerate internal injustice merits serious consideration in the United Nations.

The double policy lesson we should have learned from the events of September 11 is that misguided priorities in strange countries not normally on our radar screen can affect us in horrible and unpredictable ways; and that our own global policies must take this reality into account.

21 THE IMPORTANCE OF THE EVERYDAY ROUTINE*

Each of our daily routines is largely beyond our own making. We have some choice, but it is the choice of circumstance. Events of the past year have brought this notion home to me.

I usually don't think very much about my routine each day. I get up, wash and shave, get dressed, generally eat three meals a day, listen to uncensored local, national, and world news on the radio as I prepare for the day, read a newspaper whose content is not dictated by the government as I have my breakfast, read other uncensored newspapers with other points of view during the day, log onto the Internet to scan the stories in a number of foreign newspapers without wondering if the authorities will block my access, and then do a job that reflects my interests and was determined by the education available to me. Each action seems no big deal. It is part of my routine based on where I live and the kind of work I do. Yet, carrying out most of these actions would be a big deal for people in many other parts of the world.

I don't want to belabor the obvious. Women cannot drive in Saudi Arabia. Young girls could not to go to school under the Taliban, and grown women could not practice their professions. Eating three meals a day is a luxury in much of Africa south of the Sahara. Reading an uncensored newspaper is impossible in most of the Middle East. It can be an adventure, rather than routine, to log on to the Internet in China. Open disagreement with the government is a prosecutable offense in many parts of the world. Higher education is a luxury reserved for the few in many countries. I can practice my religion, or no religion, as I please and not be subjected to theocratic despotism. I take my civil liberties for granted, and this is why I am concerned about their curtailment in the name of fighting terrorism. Important freedoms manifest themselves in a routine of unspectacular activities that are by no means routine when these freedoms are lacking.

In somewhat similar fashion, productive relations between countries generally manifest themselves in small actions that reflect larger understandings between them.

The North American Free Trade Agreement was a major accomplishment, probably the most important agreement concluded by Mexico since

---

* *Issues in International Political Economy*, no. 33 (September 2002).

the Treaty of Guadalupe Hidalgo in February 1848 that forced the country to cede half its territory to the United States. Yet NAFTA works as it should only if goods and people can cross the border with relative ease. Most of the one million legal daily border crossings into the United States from Mexico and Canada are routine, but the ability to do this in such large numbers is spectacular. Indeed, it is probably unique in its dimension in the world.

The amount in remittances that people of Mexican origin living in the United States send to families back home is approaching $10 billion this year. Due to competition among intermediaries introduced only over the past year or so, the cost of doing this has gone down. Each remittance is a routine undertaking, but the more money the recipients get without excessive skimming by intermediate institutions is obviously a matter of great significance.

Examples of the importance of small actions can be multiplied endlessly. Countries seek tourists to develop their economies but then hassle the visitors when they seek to enter. The motor vehicle bureau of Washington, D.C., can be a nightmare because of the long delays, whereas the experience would hardly be noticed if it were routine. This kind of frustrating delay is the norm to obtain almost any kind of service from bureaucracies in developing countries. We can normally get governmental services without bribing officials, which is not the case in much of the world. Many products are produced jointly in the United States and other countries, but this works well only if there are understandings to make the parts produced in each place compatible. If the small things are not in place, the big programs are easily destroyed.

The thrust of the comments here thus far is that we are able to enjoy a simple, satisfying routine as individuals only if the big things are in place first, like democracy. We can interact routinely with people of other countries only after the larger framework is established. North and South Koreans cannot cross the border except as the two countries allow, as established by complex agreements. East Germans could not move easily into West Germany until the country was reunified. Americans, Canadians, and Mexicans can travel throughout all of North America because that is the nature of the three systems, and this movement was abetted by NAFTA.

The issue I wish to raise here is whether the direction can be changed, that is, to start with the routine small things and see if that can lead to accomplishing the bigger things. Ping-pong matches facilitated the movement toward mutual recognition between the United States and China. The documentary on the Buenavista Social Club brought Cuban music to a large audience, and this altered the attitude of many Americans toward the Cuban people. If Americans were able to travel to Cuba at will, as they can to Mexico, would this help to undermine the closed nature of the Cuban polity? A majority of the U.S. House of Representatives believes that it would, as evidenced by the approval of a bill to this effect.

The question I am raising can be put another way: Can people-to-people diplomacy play havoc with the positions of rigid governments? This diplomacy can take the form of cultural events, sporting activities, visits back and forth, e-mail chat rooms, academic conferences, and many other actions in which people interact with each other. It is clear that rewarding routine activities can be made possible by important agreements between countries, but the opportunities for these agreements are infrequent. My instinct is that the reverse is also true, that simple gestures can lead to important changes in relations between countries.

One question that is now much debated in op-ed columns is whether the majority of people who live in closed societies would welcome having the simple freedoms that people in democratic societies enjoy. I have to believe they would, but this is by no means certain. This belief was reinforced by the way the majority of Afghanis welcomed the overthrow of the Taliban. High officials in the U.S. government talk about the great service we would render to the Iraqi people if Saddam Hussein were removed from power; pundits often even argue that Saddam could be replaced by a democratic regime, after a modest lapse. Maybe, but this is most uncertain. In this view of the world, the animosity toward the United States in the Middle East would dissipate once these countries begin to enjoy freedoms they do not now have. This is thinking that starts with big things—a regime change leading to freer societies—in the hope that these great transformations might give people the ability to follow a daily routine that is similar to the one described in the opening paragraph.

Another policy path is also possible, namely, to start with the little things in our relations with Arab nations, other Muslim countries, and politically closed regimes in general. This path is not possible in the regime change aspect of U.S. policy toward Iraq, but that is probably a unique situation. The kinds of things that could be done include more cultural interchange: beaming music, rather than outright propaganda, to the people of these countries; exhibiting the work of their artists in the United States and the work of U.S. artists there; sponsoring visits of cultural and intellectual figures to and from the countries; putting together conferences on nonpolitical subjects; organizing sports competition with athletes from these countries; and other activities of this nature. Doing these small things would not be costly. They are worth a try.

PART THREE

POLICY AMBIGUITY

MIGRATION AND SANCTIONS

There are some issues for which policy direction is most uncertain, and this section contains essays on two such issues: U.S. policy on immigration and economic sanctions. Each of these issues is important and durable. Each deals with problems that are never solved but rather worked at or managed.

For those immersed in the policy aspects of these two issues, little that is conceptually new emerges with the passage of time. What one deals with are new circumstances that change the salience of the issue. In the case of migration, these changes have to do with the condition of the U.S. economy—whether it is prospering or stagnant, the number of entrants into the labor force based on earlier fertility rates, the state of relations with sending countries, and the power of competing interest groups. Shortly after Vicente Fox was elected president of Mexico in 2000, there were intense talks between the U.S. and Mexican governments about mutual agreement on immigration policy, but this discussion has subsided since the September 11, 2001, terrorist attack in the United States.

There are many significant U.S. interest groups concerned with immigration. They include businesses and employers in economic activities that seek migrants, organized U.S. labor, and Hispanic organizations (in that most low-skilled migrants now come from Latin America and the Caribbean—LAC). Some business groups want skilled or trained immigrants able to function effectively in the computer industry, or nurses. Most of these immigrants do not come from LAC countries but rather from places like India and the Philippines. Other employers seek lower-skill immigrants, such as workers for farms, hotels, restaurants, and construction. The wages offered to different classes of immigrants obviously vary, but the norm for wages for immigrant workers is lower than would have to be paid to nationals legally resident in the United States. This is a matter of much importance to organized U.S. labor; the AFL-CIO would like to legalize or regularize undocumented immigrants already in the United States because they can then more easily be unionized, thereby raising their wages. But the AFL-CIO opposes temporary guest workers, who are less amenable to unionization.

The clamor for economic sanctions at any particular time depends on what is happening in potential target countries, whether there are new manifestations of human rights violations and political repression, and the ability of the United States to secure allies willing to cooperate in the imposition of sanctions. Additional sanctions were imposed recently against Burma (Myanmar) for its renewed suppression of political rights.

It is evident that when the United States alone imposes economic sanctions—usually prohibiting imports from the offending country, limiting goods that can be sent there, and putting restrictions on investment by U.S. nationals—such actions lose their effectiveness if others continue to do business as usual. U.S. unilateralism in the field of economic sanctions, unfortunately, is the norm. Other countries generally argue that engagement with an offending country is more productive in changing behavior than cutting off economic relations. The general thrust of U.S. foreign policy today is to act more unilaterally than in the recent past, as was evident in the case of Iraq—and, in this case, this went beyond economic sanctions to open warfare, supported by few cooperating countries, to bring about regime change.

Immigration policy is not an abstraction in that it has a direct effect on people, and not just via the exchange of goods and services. Policy is ambiguous because the United States goes to great expense to keep out persons who have not been given permission to enter the country, while at the same time tolerating their long-term residence when they succeed in overcoming the obstacles placed on their entry. There are now an estimated 9 million to 10 million undocumented immigrants living in the United States, many with families and children who are U.S. citizens, and it is evident that all of these cannot be deported. It makes no economic sense to prevent them from obtaining an education or working to support their families, because they would then become an unbearable burden on the U.S. economy.

About half of these semiclandestine residents are Mexican, who have come for economic reasons as well as social unification with family and kinsmen. They now send about $12 billion a year in remittances to family and relatives in Mexico, which is an important source of foreign exchange for Mexico. Ambiguity is too mild a term when contemplating what actions to take with respect to these undocumented residents. In practice, what has happened is to leave bad enough alone, despite the agitation of many policy players and observers to do something—almost anything—sometimes harsh and, from other advocates, actions that are more accommodating.

One of the main downsides of the use of economic sanctions is that these have their impact not just on offending governments but also on the vulnerable populations in these countries. The powerful in rogue or oppressive countries can usually find ways to cope with U.S. trade restrictions, but those already poverty-stricken cannot. Pope John Paul II made this point quite forcefully when he visited Cuba in 1998.

As one might expect, an extensive network of policy centers, think tanks, and lobbying institutions has developed to opine and agitate on these two issues. Some adamantly oppose much immigration and wish to take vigorous action against the presence of illegal aliens, while others argue that the U.S.-Mexican, and to a large extent U.S.-Caribbean, labor markets are one and the same. The United States has a shortage of certain types of workers, while Mexico (and Haiti, the Dominican Republic, and others) have an excess of such workers. The debate between those advocating these competing positions is fierce, and this obviously affects the U.S. political process. The outcomes vary depending on the circumstances. Each outcome has its longer-term consequences, but the bigger story goes on much as before.

Much the same is true about the use of unilateral U.S. economic sanctions. Some endure seemingly forever, such as those directed against Cuba under Castro, and the intensity of other sanctions waxes and wanes with the changing context. Here again, actions taken have their consequences, but the larger debate seems endless and repetitive.

22   CLASHING PRESSURES ON IMMIGRATION[*]

The executive council of the AFL-CIO made a stunning shift in its position on immigration last month when it called for legalization of undocumented aliens in the United States and an end to sanctions against employers who knowingly hire them. There are now an estimated six million illegal immigrants in the United States, a majority from Mexico.

The new policy stance has contradictory aspects—one tending to raise wages and the other to lower them. For the illegal immigrants already working here, most of them unskilled, removing their clandestine status and bringing them into labor unions should raise their wages. However, the invitation to foreign workers to flock into the United States will in the future likely place downward pressure on the wages of comparable workers already here. This second aspect implies that too few U.S. nationals are expected to seek jobs in unionized industries and services and that the unions are seeking future immigrant recruits.

The AFL-CIO is not alone in seeking to attract foreign workers:

- At the urging of technology companies, the U.S. Congress keeps raising the number of individuals with high-tech training who are invited as "guest" workers. These supposedly temporary workers are likely to stay indefinitely. Indians dominate among the recipients of these H–1B visas.

- Alan Greenspan, chairman of the Federal Reserve Board, testifying before the Senate Banking Committee in January, said that despite the enormous problems associated with shifts in immigration policy, gradual changes are needed to attract qualified workers.

- The *Economist*, using data from the United Nations Population Division, concluded in an article this past January that declining fertility rates (average lifetime births per woman) will make it necessary to attract a substantial number of immigrants into Europe to keep the working population steady. The population replacement fertility rate is 2.1 and it has fallen below this in all major European countries.

[*] *Issues in International Political Economy*, no. 3 (March 2000).

- The fertility rate in Japan is now 1.5, and unless there is an increase in the years ahead, Japan's population will fall by two-thirds over the course of the twenty-first century. The problems of low fertility are compounded by the aging of populations in the industrial countries. A recent CSIS report on global aging brought out many of the implications of this reality.[1] The number of working taxpayers supporting each recipient of a public pension will fall sharply in all key industrial countries unless there is an increase in immigration. Even now, the figures are low—2.6 persons in Japan, 2.5 in France, 2.3 in Germany, and 1.3 in Italy. In 50 years, if there are no changes, the worker/pensioner ratios will fall by about one-half for these countries. The fertility decline and the worker/pensioner ratio are cause for concern in the United States, but not to the same degree as in other industrial countries because of a steady stream of immigrants.

- This combination—declining fertility and population aging—means that public pension deficits could consume all current savings of the developed world in 30 to 40 years. This projection from the Organization for Economic Cooperation and Development (OECD) assumes that all else will remain the same, but this cannot be. Something will have to give—taxes, spending, or the pension systems. The other change that may occur is acceptance of more immigrants by the industrial countries. This may not be easy to achieve, even if sought, because fertility rates are declining as well in developing countries. The fertility rate in Mexico, the main source of immigrants into the United States, is currently about replacement level, but this may not endure for more than another decade or two.

This clash in immigration policy stems from a general sentiment in the developed countries to limit new entrants at the same time that a clear need is developing for more immigrants. An article in the *Wall Street Journal* on January 17, 2000, spelled out the great effort it took for a German software entrepreneur to employ a skilled Russian programmer. More seriously, there were riots in southern Spain in February when Spaniards rampaged against Moroccan and other African workers, beating many and setting their shanties on fire. Yet, it was not too many years ago that many Spaniards benefited from their ability to migrate to higher-income European countries. The attraction of Jörg Haider's Freedom Party in Austria owes much to its anti-immigrant position.

The same is true of the popularity of the ultranationalist Jean Marie Le Pen in France. Japan has long been adamant about preserving its ethnic homogeneity by stringently limiting legal immigration. Much of Pat Buchanan's support in the United States comes from his anti-immigrant stance.

The decline in fertility rates is generally welcome in that this reduces the pressure on countries to feed and educate their populations, although this positive aspect is attenuated by the fact that fertility rates remain high in the poorest countries. There is no doubt, however, that the fertility decline and the aging of populations in the industrial countries are putting strains on workforce replacement, pensions, and public health systems. This situation is still abstract—statistical more than personal—for national populations in most industrial countries. Majority sentiment in these countries still favors limiting immigration.

It will not take too many years, however, for a full realization of the implications of fertility decline in the industrial countries. Pension and social security benefits systems will become less generous. Workforce demands will become more pressing. If there are labor shortages, economic growth will slow. The projected surpluses in the U.S. federal budget will be eaten up by health and social security costs unless these are made less generous. The increasing need for immigrants is a most unwelcome development to the national majorities in the industrial countries that favor less immigration, but reality may force a shift from an emphasis on techniques of exclusion to criteria for inclusion.

Note

[1] CSIS Global Aging Initiative, *Global Aging: The Challenge of the New Millennium* (Washington, D.C.: CSIS/Watson Wyatt, 2000). See also three studies by Robert Stowe England, director of research for the Global Aging Initiative, published by CSIS in 2002: *The Fiscal Challenge of an Aging Industrial World; Global Aging and Financial Markets—Hard Landings Ahead?* and *The Macroeconomic Impact of Global Aging—A New Era of Economic Frailty?*

23   MASSACHUSETTS' SECONDARY BOYCOTTS AGAINST BURMA*

The Supreme Court last month heard oral arguments in the case of Natsios v. National Foreign Trade Council (NFTC) on whether the Commonwealth of Massachusetts has the constitutional right to conduct a secondary boycott against companies that do business with Burma (or Myanmar, as it is currently called). Massachusetts is appealing a ruling of the federal appeals court in Boston that the commonwealth's Burma law intruded impermissibly on the federal power to conduct foreign policy. The attorney presenting the case for Massachusetts argued that a state has the power to control its own tax funds in the absence of a specific provision in the U.S. Constitution prohibiting the state and local governments from pursuing separate strategies in matters of this nature.

The case is an important one and has attracted considerable domestic and foreign interest. Although the federal government did not make the original challenge to the Massachusetts law, it did submit an amicus brief supporting the NFTC and the solicitor general did make oral arguments in which he stressed that Massachusetts was violating the foreign commerce clause by undermining national uniformity in the conduct of foreign trade. He pointed out that the U.S. government, because of its concern over human rights violations and suppression of democracy by the Burmese regime, sought to bring about change by prohibiting new investment in Burma by U.S. companies.

I am an economist and was impressed by the economic salience of many of the questions raised by the justices—all of whom spoke except Justice Clarence Thomas. I had been struck by an op-ed column by Akhil Reed Amar, a professor of constitutional law at Yale Law School, in the *Washington Post* on March 19, a few days before the Supreme Court heard oral arguments. Amar's central theme was that states have sovereignty over how to spend their tax dollars, just as private citizens can decide for themselves how to spend their disposable income. I was more impressed, however, that the column did not refer to Massachusetts' use of secondary boycotts.

Justice Stephen Breyer, in his questioning of the attorney for Massachusetts, brought out that Burma hardly competed directly for the

---

* *Issues in International Political Economy*, no. 4 (April 2000).

roughly $2 billion in annual purchases by the commonwealth and that the case, consequently, dealt with punishing secondary targets, namely the private companies that did business with Burma. Several dozen of the NFTC's 550 members were among the 346 companies on the restricted purchase list. Justice Breyer asked whether states could restrict purchases from other U.S. states if they disagreed with certain policies, such as the existence or absence of right-to-work laws. Justice Ruth Bader Ginsburg stressed the adverse foreign policy consequences of Massachusetts' law in several of her questions.

A key contention of Massachusetts was that if Congress disapproved of a state's boycott, it could enact legislation overturning the action. It was pointed out that this was not practical because there are some 39,000 separate governmental entities in the United States. At present, more than 25 states, counties, or municipalities have statutes imposing sanctions against particular foreign countries. Justice John Paul Stevens countered that Congress could enact a general law explicitly prohibiting states and localities from acting independently on such sanctions, but it is by no means evident that simple and straightforward legislation of this type is feasible—or is necessary if the Constitution inherently contains this prohibition.

CSIS published the findings of three related studies on unilateral economic sanctions and the United States (the federal government) last year.[1] The main conclusion of these studies was that when foreign countries commit grievous and offensive actions, U.S. policy—except in rare cases—is most effective when based on engagement, not isolation. When it is not possible to secure widespread support for sanctions from our allies, unilateral boycotts are unlikely to achieve any change in the behavior of the target country, and such actions also punish U.S. companies to the benefit of foreign companies. When sanctions are imposed based on domestic political grounds rather than the pursuit of U.S. foreign policy objectives, this clearly diminishes their acceptance by friendly foreign countries.

One important additional recommendation of the CSIS final report on unilateral economic sanctions on unilateral econonomic sanctions was to avoid extraterritorial application of U.S. sanctions because this angers allies more than it punishes the offending country. During his presentation, Seth Waxman, the solicitor general, made this point more dramatically when he noted the protests of the European Union against the Massachusetts law: "[t]he question now is not what to do about Burma but what to do about Massachusetts."

It cannot be disputed that foreign policy is most effective when the United States speaks with a single voice. Akhil Amar implicitly accepted this when he wrote that Massachusetts must remain free to condemn Burma "even if this makes life a little harder for the State Department." Why the State Department and not the United States? Extraterritoriality clearly angers our closest allies. It is also accepted that sanctions are most powerful in exerting economic pressure on an offending country when applied multilaterally, as in the case of Iraq (and even there, the effectiveness was diminished by the cracks in the embargo). In the case of Burma, even as the U.S. government restricted new investment, companies from other countries made new investments. Unilateral U.S. sanctions can alter a target country's behavior only when they have limited objectives, and only when they deprive a target country of something that only the United States can offer. The Massachusetts law, and others like it, deprive Burma of very little because the targets are third parties.

The United States is more prone than other countries to apply sanctions unilaterally. This past year has been remarkably free of such measures, in part because of the recognition that they rarely succeed in altering a target country's behavior. However, a big test of U.S. unilateralism is scheduled for next month when Congress takes up legislation to grant China permanent normal trading relations. If China is able to enter the World Trade Organization without U.S. support, which is a distinct possibility, this will result in discrimination against U.S. products and services exported to China because they will face higher barriers than those of other countries.

Unilateralism in trade policy has its costs whether practiced at the federal, state, or local level. Sovereign countries have the right to act against their own economic interest. A key question in the Massachusetts-Burma case is whether an individual state has the right to act against the economic and foreign policy interests of the United States as a whole.

Note

[1] Douglas Johnston and Sidney Weintraub, *Altering U.S. Sanctions Policy: Final Report of the CSIS Project on Unilateral Economic Sanctions*; Joseph J. Collins and Gabrielle D. Bowdoin, *Beyond Unilateral Economic Sanctions: Better Alternatives for U.S. Foreign Policy*; and Ernest H. Preeg, *Feeling Good or Doing Good with Sanctions: Unilateral Economic Sanctions and the U.S. National Interest* (Washington, D.C.: CSIS, 1999).

24 THE CONUNDRUM OF UNDOCUMENTED IMMIGRATION*

A campaign is under way for the United States to establish a sizeable temporary worker program—what the Europeans used to call "guest workers" and the United States, focusing on the agricultural sector during and after World War II, called the *bracero* program. Pressure is coming from two directions, from within the United States and from Mexico. The principal U.S. advocates are fruit and vegetable growers, abetted by hotel and restaurant owners, building contractors, companies that hire workers for office cleaning, and others, under the group name of Essential Worker Immigration Coalition. Vicente Fox of Mexico, shortly after he was elected president last year, floated the idea of an open border between Mexico and the United States, but then qualified this by advocating a temporary worker program until such time—perhaps 20 or so years from now—when per capita incomes in the two countries are more equal.

Advocates of these programs began their campaign when the U.S. economy was stronger than it is now, and this change may diminish popular and congressional support. Not all the proposals are alike. Agricultural growers would like a system under which temporary farm workers could become permanent residents, depending on hours worked over a number of years. Many in the Congress who favor a temporary worker program want to include provisions in any legislation to make it hard for temporary workers to remain in the United States. The Mexican authorities support an amnesty program to legalize undocumented immigrants who have been in the United States for many years, something similar to what was done under the Immigration Reform and Control Act (IRCA) of 1986. This led to substantial further immigration as family members joined those legalized under amnesty.

The executive committee of the AFL-CIO now favors something similar, to cease deporting undocumented immigrants in the United States, and also to end the program that was supposed to penalize employers for knowingly hiring illegal immigrants. Other advocacy groups have suggested carving out special provisions for Mexicans and

---

* *Issues in International Political Economy*, no. 17 (May 2001).

Canadians to obtain permanent immigrant visas based on the argument that they are land neighbors with which the United States has a free-trade agreement.

This commentary does not have enough space to cover all these and related issues. What I intend to do, instead, is to note the inconsistencies in many of the suggestions. This makes it hard for me to take an unequivocal position. My purpose is to fill in the blanks that the ardent advocates of new programs omit.

One of the most important arguments of those who want a large worker program with Mexico is that what is actually happening—the arrival and use of many Mexican workers in low-skilled positions—be made legal. Omitted is that, unless the program encompasses all who want to come, say, about a million persons a year, much illegality will continue.

Mexicans tend to chafe at border fences and other obstacles put in the way of migrants. So do many Americans, for a variety of reasons—such as dislike of a fence between friendly neighbors and forcing many border crossers to shift to dangerous locations not effectively patrolled, such as the Arizona desert, which over the past year has led to close to 500 deaths. Yet, the logic of a temporary worker program that allows legal entry to, say, 250,000 workers a year—or any number significantly less than those who want to come—is that the next step will be to reinforce the U.S. border in order to prevent undocumented entries from overwhelming the legal crossings.

Most proposals are for a temporary worker program with Mexico, as the largest source of undocumented immigrants. Does this mean that Caribbeans and Central Americans should not be given comparable, proportionate treatment?

The proposal to make special arrangements for increased permanent immigrant visas for Mexicans and Canadians raises the same issue. In recent years, legal immigrant admissions of Mexicans have been about 20 percent of the total (131,000 out of 660,000 in fiscal year 1998, the last year for which the Immigration and Naturalization Service has provided official data). Should this proportion be increased?

Other advocates of a worker program have talked about a bargain under which Mexico would seek, on its side of the border, to limit undocumented entries to the United States. Mexico has said that it would vigorously seek out and prosecute the *coyotes* who facilitate illegal entries, at a price, and would try to curtail illegal entrants into Mexico from

Central America, many of whom continue on to the United States. These measures would only scratch the surface of the problem, and Mexico may wish to take these steps in its own interest. One other suggestion is that Mexico should prevent the *exit* of those of its citizens who do not have visas to enter the United States. Would President Fox want to be remembered as the president who prevented Mexicans from leaving the country in a way akin to what the East Germans did before unification? It is hard to believe that serious Americans would want a friendly and democratic neighbor to do that.

The deep belief of most migration researchers, based on past experience, is that temporary residence of foreign workers inevitably leads to large-scale permanent residence. One way suggested to prevent this is to put a significant portion of the salaries of temporary workers (say, 25 percent) into a forced savings account to be returned with interest on departure from the country. Does the United States really want to enter into this modern form of indenture? What happens to the money if the person does not leave the United States? Do we want to reduce the migrant's ability to send remittances to his or her family?

We are regularly assured by advocates of temporary programs that the workers take jobs nobody else wants and, therefore, workers legally in the United States suffer no damage. We know from research that previous immigrant cohorts with similar skills do suffer. However, the underlying argument is that few want these jobs at such low wages. Should national U.S. policy be based on the assurance of subnormal wages for foreigners in specified industries?

Advocates of foreign worker programs meet the foregoing argument by citing the position of the AFL-CIO to cease deportations of undocumented immigrants and to forget about the fines mandated by the IRCA. The AFL-CIO position presumably is based on the desire of some of its unions to organize workers in low-paying activities. Why is it preferable to have undocumented workers come to low-wage jobs in the United States in industries that will inevitably need protection as opposed to having these workers stay home and then importing what they produce without excessive protection?

I could continue, but I think my point is clear. There are ambiguities in the advocacy of temporary worker programs that benefit particular U.S. interests at the expense of a coherent national immigration policy. The late Barbara Jordan, when she chaired the Commission on Immigration Reform, argued in favor of immigration to the United States, but legally, through the front door. Yet, the reality is that much immigration comes clandestinely, abetted by a variety of U.S. interests. The persons who come are courageous risk takers, filled with initiative to improve their lot in life and that of their families. I instinctively join with Barbara Jordan's position, but I know that what is happening is different. This disparity between the reality of illegal immigration and respecting a legal queue is what makes this such a hard issue about which to fashion policy.

25 SANCTIONS: WHEN THEY DON'T WORK, KEEP DOING THE SAME*

I long ago realized that one way for the CEO of a large corporation to get a big bonus was to get fired. For a top government official, a well-trodden path for moving up is to thoroughly mess up the current job. The surefire way for unilateral sanctions to endure is to fail in their primary objective. If they haven't worked, that proves they are still needed, even if sometimes the implicit objective has to be revised.

The poster case demonstrating this point on the durability of sanctions is Cuba. Relations between Cuba and the United States deteriorated rapidly after Castro seized power and the United States put a trade embargo in place in early 1962. The original rationale was to safeguard national security, which we learned during the missile crisis with the Soviet Union in 1962 had some merit. The operational purpose was to punish Cuba so severely as to lead to Castro's overthrow. The national security basis for the embargo has since disappeared, but the embargo continues with a variety of modifications, some easing the restrictions and others tightening them.

The most prominent aspect of the current version of sanctions is contained in the Helms-Burton, or Libertad, Act (formally the Cuban Liberty and Democratic Solidarity Act of 1996). Title III of this legislation permits lawsuits in U.S. courts against foreign companies that traffic in property confiscated by Cuba from U.S. citizens and from others who were not then U.S. citizens, but have since become so. It is this title that President Bush recently waived, as President Clinton had many times before. The purpose of the embargo is still punishment—but apparently for its own sake.

The U.S. economic sanctions against Cuba are not unique, even if the durability is. Other examples of unilateral sanctions—of the United States acting alone without the support of allies—are in place against Iran, Libya, North Korea, Sudan, and Burma. The sanctions against Iraq started multilaterally, but have since lost the support of many other countries. It was this failure to obtain the continued cooperation of

---

* *Issues in International Political Economy*, no. 20 (August 2001).

other countries that stimulated Secretary of State Colin Powell to suggest a new approach, and to try to sell it by using alliterative exaggeration—namely, the idea of "smart sanctions." The "smart" aspect of the proposal was to target the punishment more directly at offensive policies adopted by Iraq's leaders rather than at the Iraqi people.

There is general agreement that comprehensive unilateral sanctions have the following shortcomings:

- Their main accomplishment is punishment.
- The punishment, as Pope John Paul II said when he visited Cuba in 1998, hurts the general population rather than the leaders who devise the offending policies.
- Business with the target country is turned over to foreign competitors, mostly in other industrial countries, and this may have long-term consequences because non-U.S. trading and investment relationships are established.
- The extraterritorial application of many U.S. sanctions laws leads to quarrels with the very countries with which cooperation is most desired on other issues.
- The economic interests of friendly, bystander countries are hurt by their inability to facilitate or carry on trade with the sanctioned country.
- U.S. prestige is diminished because its policies are unsuccessful.
- Incentives for smuggling prohibited goods are created.

If there is general acceptance of these shortcomings of comprehensive unilateral sanctions, why then is the United States so persistent in pursuing them? Supporters of unilateral sanctions surely do not wish to punish people in target countries just for the sake of punishment. One must assume, also, that supporters of economic sanctions are just as rational as the opponents. Why, then, the deep differences in outlook?

There are four categories of explanations for the positions of the supporters of unilateral sanctions. The first is that domestic politics trumps foreign policy. This is particularly germane for Cuba. But this explanation has more widespread application, in that politicians prefer to be seen doing something rather than standing by when the actions of other countries are seen as reprehensible. The second is that U.S. economic sanctions, which may deprive Iran and Libya of resources, limit their ability to export terrorism. Perhaps, but this argument loses force as long as the two countries are recipients of non-U.S. investment and are able to earn ample resources from oil exports. The third contention of sanctions advocates is that the refusal to grant access to the U.S. market may push target countries to improve the human rights of its nationals. This was the basis for the opposition to granting permanent normal trading relations to China. In the end, the opposition did not carry the day. This was not a glorious victory for principle; denying U.S. exporters and investors access to the small Cuban market was acceptable, but not to the potentially immense Chinese market.

The fourth and main argument of the proponents of unilateral sanctions is that there is no better way for the United States to express its distaste for the behavior of target countries. It would be preferable if all sanctions could be carried out multilaterally, but other industrial countries will not normally cooperate in this action. Economic sanctions were devised initially as a superior alternative to military action—although, in Cuba, the failed Bay of Pigs invasion preceded the economic embargo.

If one strips away the rhetoric—and if the United States is unable to persuade other countries to join in the economic sanctions—there are essentially only two other options to unilateral sanctions. The first is smart sanctions, namely, to pinpoint the sanctions against the leaders of the target country or against some specific action, such as when the target country sells technology that enables a third country to produce weapons of mass destruction. A targeted sanction removes the comprehensive aspect of the U.S. action. There are examples of successful targeted sanctions, although the record overall is not illustrious. For that matter, the success record of multilateral sanctions is limited—perhaps to the South African case in the international struggle to end apartheid; and even there, the sanctions did not stand alone. As we are now witnessing, the multilateral sanctions against Iraq are breaking down.

The second alternative is engagement—or, to add a desirable adjective, constructive engagement. The proponents of unilateral sanctions argue that engagement does not work—or does not work any better than do comprehensive unilateral sanctions. This, however, is unknowable, unless pursued for a long enough time. Authoritarian governments with which the United States was engaged in East Asia have become democracies, such as South Korea and Taiwan. Economic-political engagement is now under way with Vietnam. It will take time to assess whether U.S. economic engagement will improve China's human rights behavior.

The United States both engaged with the Soviet Union and its satellites and practiced targeted sanctions—behavior quite distinct from that employed against Cuba since the embargo—and, over time, there were profound changes. These changes surely were not the result of engagement alone, but there is no gainsaying that engagement was part of U.S. policy.

The record of engagement leading to significant changes in the policies of countries that might also be targets of comprehensive unilateral sanctions is mixed. By contrast, the record of comprehensive unilateral sanctions in changing the behavior of target countries is uniformly negative.

26 MIGRATION: MAKING POLICY IN THE FACE OF PROFOUND DISAGREEMENT*

Migration is a perennial subject, one that deals with a basic aspect of human existence. The intensity of the debate, however, varies with the times. Migration is a hot issue when the economy of the receiving country is weak, or when the political situation in the sending country is in turmoil. It was an excruciatingly difficult problem when India and Pakistan, on religious grounds, became two countries, and in Rwanda, as the Hutus and Tutsis set about killing each other. Ireland and Italy, for much of their histories, produced too many people for the size of their economies, and emigration was the solution. Japan today is producing too few people, and the opposition to immigration is increasingly becoming the problem there.

Migration is primarily an economic phenomenon, but obviously has political, religious, ethnic, familial, and labor manifestations. These are dismal times in many parts of the world, and it is thus no accident that migration issues are proliferating. The European Union recently held a meeting in Seville whose purpose was to find ways to limit immigration. But for the strong opposition of France and Sweden, the EU might have adopted a dreadful resolution to impose economic sanctions against states that were the source of illegal immigration. The United Nations held a conference last week that was stimulated by a similar concern, namely, the large flow of illegal immigration. There has been much publicity in recent weeks highlighting both Western European and American fears of terrorist immigration. The United States and Canada recently reached agreement to make asylum seekers ask for refuge in the first country they come to with the purpose of limiting shopping around. A migration understanding with the United States that Mexico thought was in the works disappeared after the events of September 11, 2001, and reviving it may be difficult.

There are some elemental features that guide national and individual sentiments. The rich countries favor unfettered movement of goods, services, and capital—but not of people. The poor countries are not ardent advocates of free trade—but they are of free movement of people,

---

* *Issues in International Political Economy*, no. 31 (July 2002).

especially if they are headed to rich countries. Those who live in crowded urban areas are all in favor of keeping people down on the farm. Those living in poverty in rural areas prefer to take their chances in the cities. The governments of migrant-sending countries argue passionately for the humane treatment of their nationals living illegally elsewhere, even as they mistreat their nationals at home. The migrant-receiving countries are vociferous in insisting that undocumented immigrants are "illegal," but they show less concern about those who live legally in poverty before they emigrate. These complexities are enough to make migration bargaining harrowing, but these difficulties are compounded in specific situations.

This essay is being written in the United States and will focus on the American situation. Similar, perhaps even more difficult, problems exist elsewhere. The United States, for many years, has consciously been a migrant-welcoming country, an attitude that is not common around the world. What this means is that the U.S. government and Congress, when they decide each year how many legal immigrants should be admitted, have been more generous than most other countries.

Other than this most basic decision of how many people to admit, the most complex immigration issue with which the United States must now deal is how to handle the reality of undocumented immigrants already here, and how to prevent or discourage others from coming without the proper papers. There are now an estimated 9 million undocumented immigrants living in the United States. Many of them live in families that are a mixture of illegals and citizens. The sheer numbers, as well as specific family situations, mean that the illegals cannot all be deported. Even if they could be found, which is problematic, such mass deportation is not something that a civilized nation, "under God," can do. The reality, therefore, is that the undocumented immigrants will remain in the United States, either legalized (or regularized, as some prefer to call it) or underground. How does one choose between these two options? If legalized, they can live normal lives; if not, they remain subject to exploitation in the country where most of them will live for the rest of their lives.

The problem with legalization (regularization) is that this gives an incentive for more people to enter the United States without documents, which they do by crossing land borders or overstaying visas. When President Vicente Fox discussed regularization with President George W. Bush before 9/11, the conversation dealt with Mexicans in the United States. U.S. foreign policy would not permit legalization just of Mexicans because there are millions of illegals from other countries. If I had to hazard a guess what action U.S. leaders will take, it would be "nothing" (i.e., live with an unsatisfactory—really, a horrible—situation for at least a generation).

The land borders with Mexico and Canada present another problem, namely, the conflict between security against terrorist entries and the efficient movement of goods. The United States wants to facilitate entry for those with proper papers—close to two million a day for the two countries combined—and to prevent the entry of terrorists, with or without documents. We want to speed the movement of goods—close to $2 billion a day in and out of the United States with our two land neighbors—entering into legitimate commerce. These are unavoidable problems that must be solved; we do not have the choice of doing nothing.

President Fox has put migration issues at the top of his agenda with the United States. The negotiation was effectively halted by the events of 9/11, but the issue has not gone away forever. In addition to the two aspects noted above—legalization and concern about terrorism—there are proposals, from both Mexican authorities and U.S. employers, for a substantial temporary or guest program for low-skilled workers, especially in agriculture. There are now an estimated 2.5 million farm workers in the United States, of which 1.2 million are undocumented, mostly from Mexico. Under normal conditions, one would expect 10 to 20 percent of farm workers to exit each year to other occupations. If this holds true in the future, this would call for about 250,000 new agricultural workers each year, practically all of whom would have to be imported. In other words, the guest worker program would be temporary only for the individuals, but would have to continue year after year—be permanent, in other words—for the United States. The question this raises is whether the ideal immigration policy for the United States is one that gives special attention, year in and year out, to meeting the desire of particular employers for low-wage workers.

All immigrant-receiving countries are grappling with a related set of issues. Accepting the reality that richer countries will not open their borders to the free entry of people—as they might for the free entry of goods, services, and capital—what procedures will they use to obtain the kinds of immigrants they want? Countries make these choices now: Canada has a point system designed to choose skilled immigrants; the

United States gives preference to family reunion, although there is also a program for skilled persons; other countries have variants of these. Receiving countries want to choose; that is why there is a general antipathy to illegal entries.

Decisions must be made on the number of immigrants wanted. This, in essence, was what led to the brouhaha at the Seville meeting of the EU. Denmark and the Netherlands, formerly seen as immigrant-friendly countries, at least relatively, have become more restrictive. As one looks objectively at the demographic trends in many developed countries, especially in Europe and Japan, one would conclude that they would want to attract immigrants. This, so far, turns out not to be the case. Emotion, not pure reasoning, dominates the decisionmaking.

Looked at in reverse, rational and adventurous people in many developing countries, where birth rates are high and educational and economic opportunities are wanting, jump at the chance to emigrate. They will do so without documentation if the documents are not forthcoming legally. This sets up deep tension that will not go away. The argument often made in the rich countries that the better option for poor countries is development is fatuous for countries where poverty is intense and the development option really asks several generations to forego better opportunities.

There are some problems that have no ideal answers. Immigration is one of these, and most countries are settling for second best—or maybe the correct description is "first worst."

PART FOUR

DEMOCRACY AND SOVEREIGNTY

There are three essays in this section, undoubtedly too few for matters as important as these. As I look back over the past four years of writing these commentaries, I plead guilty to underemphasizing these two themes.

The central argument in the following sovereignty paper is that the principle is all too frequently invoked hypocritically. This is true in the United States, as it is in other countries. Samuel Johnson alerted us long ago to this inherent dishonesty, although the word he used was "patriotism."

Mexican politicians shouted "protection of sovereignty" until recently as the reason for not discussing migration matters with the U.S. government. Ostensibly, they were protecting the U.S. sovereign right to decide these matters on its own, although another motive was to dissuade the United States from getting deeply into internal Mexican issues—whether migration, protection of human rights, the nature of the authoritarian regime, or trade and investment restrictions against foreigners. The United States regularly invokes sovereignty when it imposes direct or indirect import restrictions, such as farm subsidies undercutting the markets of more efficient producers. The United States, exercising its sovereign right, consciously violated an explicit obligation it undertook in NAFTA when it disallowed Mexican trucks from carrying goods from Mexico into and across the United States on the grounds that both the trucks and the drivers were unreliable.

There has been a long although not necessarily straight-line process of expanding the sharing of sovereignty. This is true in the trade field, as countries exchange obligations and benefits. The suppression of human rights within countries is no longer an inalienable right of national oppressive governments. Environmental protection is recognized as a global responsibility. Even national defense, the sine qua non of sovereignty, has become a shared responsibility—as in the North American Treaty Organization. The current U.S. government has spurned much of this sharing of sovereignty in the environmental and defense fields, but my expectation is that this situation will revert to the trend of sharing responsibilities at some point.

The main theme of the democracy paper that follows is that there is a relationship between competitive markets and democracy. There is no iron rule that competitive markets necessarily lead to democratic political regimes, but it is clear that government-operated and -controlled economies are invariably authoritarian or dictatorial. Any number of nations moved from authoritarianism to democracy in recent decades—South Korea, Taiwan, and, more recently, Mexico. One reason, I believe, is that when economic decisionmaking is highly decentralized, this builds up pressure for seeking decentralized choice in the political arena as well. Will China, which increasingly is achieving a market system of economics, move in the direction of greater political democracy? The very fact that speculation about this transformation exists demonstrates a widespread belief that this is a natural sequence. It is impossible to predict the tipping point, but it is clear that the status quo is not an equilibrium situation and therefore cannot endure.

The Latin American and Caribbean region is emphasized in the essays in this book. Democracy has been an elusive objective in this region for historical and social reasons. Markets exist in the LAC region, but they have been highly imperfect; there has been much government domination as well as oligopolistic business activity. The LAC societies have been, and frequently still are, highly polarized by income, level of education, and access to vital services, such as health care, shelter, and food. However, there was a substantial shift in governance from military and authoritarian regimes during the past two decades. Democracy, although often fragile, is now the norm. Cuba is the big exception. Overt overthrow of elected regimes is now anathema, and the region has acted collectively to prevent this in at least one case, that of Paraguay in 1989. The issue in the LAC region is no longer the attainment of democracy, but its maintenance and strengthening. This is a significant change since the 1980s.

27 CHEAPENING THE SOVEREIGNTY ARGUMENT*

There is a tendency in the United States to invoke sovereignty as the reason for rejecting international initiatives that are opposed on other grounds. The demonstrations in Seattle against the World Trade Organization and in Washington, D.C., against the International Monetary Fund and the World Bank raised the sovereignty issue in castigating decisionmaking in these organizations. The International Financial Institution Advisory Commission (the Meltzer Commission) asserted that conditions on long-term loans from the IMF to developing countries "undermined national sovereignty" and thereby hindered democratic development; the commission could have given legitimate reasons for discontinuing such lending. Ralph Nader and Public Citizen argue vigorously that globalization and its primary mechanisms (the WTO and NAFTA) are designed to benefit corporations, thereby compromising democracy; the upshot of the Public Citizen argumentation, however, ends up as protectionism. Pat Buchanan is the most unequivocal of sovereigntists in his desire to shield the United States from imports of goods and immigrants he considers undesirable.

Many individuals and institutions that bemoan the loss of U.S. independence in economic matters are prepared to ignore sovereignty when it comes to the political and social behavior of other countries. The failure to respect internationally recognized human rights was a major argument in the effort to reject permanent normal trade relations for China. Secondary boycotts are used against foreign corporations that do business with Cuba even though U.S. allies consider this an infringement of their sovereignty. President Fujimori of Peru was attacked by the U.S. government for the irregularities in his recent re-election, but little support came from important Latin American countries, especially Brazil and Mexico, which were loath to interfere in Peru's internal affairs.

The use of the sovereignty argument is clearly selective and idiosyncratic by country. It has become almost synonymous with import protection in the United States, whereas lesser powers ordinarily invoke sovereignty to counter alleged interference in their internal affairs. Our

* *Issues in International Political Economy*, no. 6 (June 2000).

closest allies—Canada and the European Union are good examples—resent what they consider U.S. extraterritoriality in the use of economic sanctions against their corporations. This all-purpose invocation of sovereignty based on circumstance depreciates the coin—few in the United States listen any more when the word is used.

There are real sovereignty issues. The choice of government, the nature of governance, defense of the national homeland, and issues of war and peace are among these. Sovereignty does not have to be specifically invoked for these matters because it is accepted as natural. There are limits, however, even in these areas. For example, most European allies have misgivings about a U.S. national missile defense because this may affect their own security. Yet, in the end, it is clear that the United States has a sovereign right to make its own decisions about its own homeland defense, even if there is a severe cost in relations with other countries.

The cheapening of the sovereignty invocation arises most forcefully when it is evident that other objectives are being pursued. This is most striking in the trade area. The United States has negotiated tariff and quota reductions in exchange for comparable reductions by other countries since the birth of the country more than two centuries ago. This kind of commitment is a sacrifice of sovereignty, but willingly entered into in exchange for the offsetting benefits it affords. National treatment is granted to foreign investors in the United States in exchange for comparable treatment by U.S. investors overseas. The United States enters into international organizations to provide a collective good that transcends national boundaries, whether this is to provide a set of rules guiding international trade or a set of protections dealing with the global environment. The United States objects when other countries play loose with these rules; we object to the refusal of the EU to admit hormone-treated beef despite the lack of evidence that it is unsafe for human consumption. Other countries react similarly when the United States does not live up to its commitments; Mexico had every right to complain when the United States, for domestic political reasons, ignored its commitment to permit free passage of trucks from Mexico six years after NAFTA went into effect (i.e., on January 1, 2000). These are acts of protection enveloped in a sovereignty argument. It is hard to run a world trading system when countries ignore obligations freely entered into.

International agreements generally have escape mechanisms. Countries have a right to impose restrictions when domestic interests are threatened by imports, but there is an expectation that agreed procedures will be followed and compensation will be offered for losses suffered by the exporting countries. Countries have a right to invoke national security considerations in order not to carry out agreements, but there is an expectation that this will not be specious, as would have been the case when the United States intimated it would use national security grounds to justify a secondary boycott with respect to Cuba. Import restrictions can be invoked on environmental grounds, but again there is an expectation that this will not be done promiscuously.

Invocation of the sovereignty excuse for policy action must also take into account the nature of the times. There was a time when countries violated the human rights of their own nationals without attracting denunciations from foreign governments or nongovernmental organizations. That time has passed. The lack of democracy was once universally recognized as an internal issue. This recognition is no longer universal. Import restrictions in order to promote domestic production was the norm in Latin America 15 to 20 years ago. It is not today, now that these countries have received reciprocal benefits from international negotiations. The globalization of markets has, in fact, been criticized more by critics in the United States, critics who regularly use the sovereignty argument, than in developing countries where increased trade is seen as an avenue of escape from grinding poverty.

The changed outlook toward the applicability of the sovereignty argument has been remarkable in recent years. When NAFTA was under negotiation, the conventional expectation was that Mexico and not the United States would raise sovereignty concerns (raising these concerns had been near automatic for Mexican politicians in their pronouncements about relations with the United States). Exactly the reverse happened. The sovereignty issue, for the most part, was muted in Mexico. It was stentorian in the United States, as it is to this day. Canada was quite vociferous about protecting its cultural sovereignty during the NAFTA negotiations, but this was a non-issue in Mexico. Many Mexican industrialists favor dollarization of the Mexican economy, discarding the peso completely. This is a real sovereignty issue in that it signifies the sacrifice of an independent monetary policy. Dollarization is seriously discussed today in Mexico and elsewhere in Latin America and the Caribbean. This is a profound indication that the old appeals to sovereignty and to patriotism as a diversion from bad economic policy are largely dissipated.

The United States is more likely to invoke sovereignty as a subterfuge for other objectives than are countries far less powerful economically and politically. There has been a transference: The weaker countries increasingly accept the realities they must confront, and the powerful United States all too frequently refuses to do so on issues that do not inherently threaten its sovereignty.

28 DEMOCRACY AND MARKETS[*]

Taiwan evolved gradually into a democracy, but China did not. South Korea is a democracy, but North Korea is still a totalitarian country. West Germany was a democracy well before unification, but East Germany was led by a dictatorial regime. The different outcomes in these three cases cannot be attributed to historical cultural conditioning, but rather to more recent political circumstances. In each case, the transition to democracy took place in a market economy, while the durability of dictatorship occurred in countries in which the state made the major economic decisions.

The foregoing three examples demonstrate a simple reality: totalitarian regimes that adopt market economics can alter the nature of their governance for the better. Democracy in each of these cases involves open elections, the alternation of political parties in power, a free press, and free speech—critical aspects of society still absent (or which were absent in East Germany) in the three sister states.

A more complex example of transformation to democracy can take the analysis further. Mexicans, on July 2 of this year, elected a new president, thereby ending 71 years of single-party rule, which will become effective when Vicente Fox is sworn in on December 1. Until recently,.Mexico has been a faux democracy, with all the paraphernalia of elections, but whose outcomes, until recently, were known in advance. Mexico had considerable individual free speech, but the media were controlled by the government through various devices. The role of the state in the economy was large, and key competitive features of the market were limited. In its way, the market structure was much like the political system, a façade that was as much fraud as reality. Market competition began slowly in the early 1980s when import restrictions were eased, then gained steam when Mexico joined the General Agreement on Tariffs and Trade in 1986, and reached an apex when free trade with the United States came into force under NAFTA in 1994. Carlos Salinas de Gortari, the president responsible for Mexico's entry into NAFTA, did not hide his priority of opening the economy before allowing the political system to become truly competitive. Ernesto Zedillo, Salinas' successor, gave his final *informe*, in effect his farewell address,

[*] *Issues in International Political Economy*, no. 9 (September 2000).

on September 1, 2000, in which his clear message was that the liberal economic policy Mexico has been following contributed importantly to Mexico's democratic transition.

One additional group of examples can be offered. The Czech Republic and Poland moved rapidly to adopt a competitive market system after Soviet dominance. Indeed, there was much criticism at the time that shock therapy for the two economies would lead to serious hardships. Romania, the Ukraine, and other former Soviet republics were slow to adopt competitive markets. Democracy is considerably more robust in the first two countries than in the others. This can be attributed in part in the Czech case to its earlier democratic history, but there can be little doubt that the Czech story would have been different absent its return to a competitive market structure.

Many analysts have pointed out that while all democracies have competitive market structures, not all countries with market economies are democratic. It is also true that not all democracies retain their competitive political systems. Russia elected its current president, but it is evident that the media are not completely free; nor are markets competitive, as the use of the word "oligarch" to describe those who have been able to manipulate the economic system attests. President Alberto Fujimori was first elected in a democratic election, but democracy in Peru has since retrogressed. So too was President Hugo Chávez elected democratically, but the future of democracy in Venezuela is uncertain. Chávez was able to exploit the populist sentiment in his country because the economy was far from being competitive and roughly 80 percent of the population lives in poverty.

President Zedillo used the word "liberal" to describe his economic policy, by which he had in mind a competitive structure and minimum government involvement in the operation of Mexico's economy, other than to set the macroeconomic framework and establish important social safeguards. The critics of this policy use the term "neoliberal" in order to imply a kind of capitalism that tolerates great income inequality and excessive poverty. Most of the demonstrators who show up to protest at international economic meetings around the world—from Seattle (the World Trade Organization), Washington, D.C. (the World Bank and the International Monetary Fund), Melbourne as this is written (an Asian economic gathering), and no doubt in Prague later this month (when the annual meetings of the World Bank and IMF convene)—take an exploitative view of markets.

Are the critics correct? They are if competitive market capitalism is equated with Darwinian economic survival—that is, with capitalism that has no social dimensions. They are correct if the authorities are unwilling to deal with corporate stifling of competition. They are correct when governments systematically favor special over national interests or tolerate crony capitalism. However, all modern industrial countries have programs to deal with the suppression of competition, that is, with interference with the workings of markets. All have safety nets, some more inclusive than others. It is hard to understand why the demonstrators in Seattle, who claim to be supporters of democracy, favored protection against competitive imports. They are working at cross purposes with themselves.

There is no assurance that the operation of markets, coupled with techniques to promote competition (both internally and from imports) and governmental mechanisms to assure social justice, will lead to the establishment of democratic institutions. On the other hand, we do know that the lack of markets—the existence of government monopolies or near monopolies over a country's economy—will not lead to democracy. The reasons for this are reasonably straightforward. Markets promote decentralized decisionmaking and the greater the competitive pressures, the more variegated this decisionmaking is.

A key argument of those who favor granting permanent normal trade relations to China follows precisely this logic—that this will decentralize economic decisionmaking in China. The reasoning is that, over time, China may follow a path similar to that of Taiwan and South Korea, resulting in the progressive opening of the political system alongside the economic structure. The alternative policy, that of restricting the development of China's market structure by rejecting normal trade relations with the United States, offers little hope for China's democratic development.

These are not sure things. Developing a competitive market does not necessarily lead to the establishment of a democratic society, but there is a positive probability that it will. This, I submit, is a chance worth taking in China and elsewhere, if we value the positive evolution of societies currently closed to outside political influences.

29 DEMOCRACY AND DEVELOPMENT*

President Bush delivered a carefully worded speech on November 6 to celebrate the twentieth anniversary of the National Endowment for Democracy. The stated theme of the talk was to extol the values of democracy and to argue that the Middle East, and Islam generally, are not "condemned by history or culture to live in despotism." The subtext was to provide a more acceptable rationale for the invasion of Iraq—namely, to secure democracy there—than the earlier one of ridding Iraq of weapons of mass destruction. In addition to this immediate motive, the president made a significant policy statement to the effect that the United States would no longer accommodate to the lack of freedom in the Middle East. We must now await future administration actions.

The president's speech had another theme, namely, that democracy and development go hand in hand. "[T]he prosperity and vitality and technological progress of a people are directly determined by [the] extent of their liberty." This is probably true once countries have passed what Walter Rostow called the takeoff stage in their development, but it may not be the norm before that point. This is an issue that has long interested those who think about the political-economic-social preconditions for development. It is a theme that arises periodically in Latin America, such as after Jeanne Kirkpatrick wrote her well-known November 1979 article in *Commentary* about the potential transformation of authoritarian governments, which led to her appointment as U.S. ambassador to the United Nations. The approach to authoritarian regimes is less relevant today in Latin America because most countries in the region are nominally democratic.

In a speech on September 17 of this year to the German Historical Institute in Washington, D.C., Helmut Schmidt, the former chancellor of Germany, said the following: "[A]mong the developing countries, only those will be the winners who are governed by economically enlightened governments that, at the same time, are governed in a strictly authoritarian way." Schmidt cited as examples China as well as what he referred to as the "four little tigers"—Singapore, Hong Kong, South Korea, and Taiwan. He said that they needed authoritarian governments for the development they had achieved over the last four decades.

---

* *Issues in International Political Economy*, no. 47 (November 2003).

In remarks to a Cato Institute seminar on June 5, 2003, on "Bringing Liberal Democracy to Iraq," Fareed Zakaria made much the same point about East Asian countries as Schmidt did about for developing countries generally. Countries like South Korea, Taiwan, Malaysia, and Thailand, he wrote, "have built the rule of law, a commercial class, an independent middle class, and *then* democracy...." (Emphasis in the original.) "Democracy," he said, "is hard work. It is very much worth trying to spread, but it takes a much broader process of modernization and liberalization than people realize."

The dictatorial Pinochet government introduced the liberal economic policies that helped make Chile the showcase country for economic development that it has been over the past 20 years. Chile enjoyed democracy before Pinochet, but the governments were not "economically enlightened," to use Schmidt's term. The democratic governments that followed Pinochet have been economically enlightened—indeed, they have kept most of the Pinochet-era economic policies. Mexico's miracle period of economic growth of 6 to 7 percent a year from 1954 until roughly the mid-1970s, with moderate inflation, took place under an authoritarian regime. Significant economic reforms were introduced in Brazil after the 1964 military coup. Latin American growth has been more stop-and-go than in East Asia, but the order of change in the more successful countries was largely as Zakaria described for East Asia—first economic reform and then liberty. None of the Latin American countries has been as economically successful over as many years as those in East and Northeast Asia.

I agree generally with Zakaria's explanation for the sequencing of economics first, then democracy: namely, that a successful democracy requires informed stakeholders, a vibrant middle class, an entrepreneurial group of risk takers, and an educated population that is prepared for—indeed, insists on—making many decisions for itself. Before these conditions are in place, a central authority that one hopes is enlightened normally makes these decisions. China, one of the countries named by Schmidt, has had economically enlightened policy leaders since Deng Xiaoping, but the democratic transition has yet to occur. The current speculation is about the timing of this transition; this type of speculation never arose before the economic transition.

Are there exceptions to this sequencing to democracy in the modern era, say, during the past century? Israel might be such a case, but it was a country populated mostly by people already educated, rather than having to develop an educated citizenry. There are other cases in which the sequencing is unclear, or moved from one aspect to the other. It is worth noting the obvious, that authoritarianism does not necessarily lead to development; indeed, in Argentina, the authoritarian regime of Juan Perón led to economic retrogression. Venezuela seems to be going in a reverse direction, moving away from democracy, accompanied by what can be called disdevelopment.

I raise these issues here because they are instructive as to what the Bush policy in Iraq should be if the end goal is democracy *and* development. Can the two take place simultaneously, or would it be preferable to favor the sequencing suggested by Schmidt and Zakaria in a country that has known precious little democracy in its recent history? Many U.S. nongovernmental organizations are now giving lessons in democratic transition in Iraq, but it is hard to believe that any of this is taking hold in the midst of the violence and economic devastation that prevail. Many of the examples given by President Bush in his speech of governments that are experimenting with changes favoring democracy support the thesis of economics first. These include Bahrain, Kuwait, Jordan, Qatar, and Morocco.

Would it be a tragedy if the coalition forces were to turn Iraq over to economically enlightened but authoritarian leaders? I raise this question not to give a definitive response, but rather as one that is worthy of debate and analysis. The Bush administration is already signaling that it will turn the governance of the country over to Iraqis sooner rather than later. The reason has little to do with what Bush said in his speech, but rather can be explained by the failure of the United States to restore order on its own and the unwillingness to send more troops to do the job. We obviously do not know in advance which leaders will be economically enlightened; nor do we know that an Iraqi leadership that professes democracy when installed will remain that way.

The 1980s were harsh years economically in Latin America, but those and subsequent years saw substantial political transformations from authoritarian and military regimes to democratic ones. This transformation was complete in all the countries in the Southern Cone and took place as well in some countries in the Andean region. The shift from authoritarianism to democracy was gradual in Mexico, but reached its apogee in 2000 when the National Action Party won the presidency after 71 years of rule by the Institutional Revolutionary Party. The main reason for the democratic rebirth in the 1980s, in my view, was the failure of the authoritarian and military regimes to deliver satisfactory rates of GDP growth. Democracy did not grow out of economically enlightened authoritarian leadership, as in East Asia, but out of economically unenlightened authoritarianism.

During the past few years, the economic failures have taken place under ostensibly democratic regimes. Is there a danger that this will lead to a return of authoritarianism in the hope of accomplishing more satisfactory rates of economic growth? The past never repeats itself precisely, but changes in many democratic regimes are in fact taking place. Democratically elected presidents are not being ousted by coups, but are being forced out of office by street demonstrations and disruptions of civic order. Some recent examples are Argentina, Peru, Ecuador, and Bolivia. The durability of democracy first and then economic growth in Latin America is clearly under challenge. This is troubling, but the silver lining is that even as democratically elected leaders are being removed by essentially nondemocratic means, the trappings of democracy are holding firm in the choice of successors in all four countries mentioned.

My purpose here is not to question the great effort the United States is making to promote democracy around the world. Anti-Americanism is growing in the aftermath of the invasion of Iraq, and there is considerable skepticism that Iraq can be transformed into a durable democracy. Yet, in Latin America, perhaps the most significant political action being taken to counteract such anti-Americanism is the pro-democracy and liberty stance of the United States. This is obviously not enough; some evidence of renewed economic growth and greater social equality would be much more effective in reducing anti-Americanism.

PART FIVE

INTER-AMERICAN RELATIONS

This section of the collected essays deals most directly with specific country and overall hemispheric political and economic situations. The papers deal with developments at the time they were written in Argentina, Brazil, Chile, Mexico, Peru, and Venezuela, plus one commentary on Canada-U.S. relations. I have missed some important countries in these writings, but all will come in good time.

As I reread the papers, a number of themes emerge. First, there is a U.S. quest for bilateral, plurilateral, and hemispheric cooperation. And there have been some important successes in this endeavor, such as the establishment of NAFTA and the recently concluded free-trade agreement with Chile. NAFTA, in my view, was the most important Mexico-U.S. agreement in this century, and perhaps the most important Mexico-U.S. agreement since the Treaty of Guadalupe-Hidalgo in the nineteenth century, which forced (it was not a voluntary pact, as was NAFTA) Mexico to cede a large part of its territory. The Chile-U.S. free trade agreement may stimulate other U.S. integration agreements in the hemisphere, including the Free Trade Area of the Americas, although this is speculative.

Second, many uncertainties exist, including the ultimate success of the FTAA negotiations and the substantive content of the U.S.-Central American FTA negotiations. These uncertainties reflect ambiguous U.S. and regional positions on free trade and how comprehensive either side wishes any agreement to be. The United States is unwilling to negotiate agricultural subsidies and trade safeguard measures (antidumping and countervailing duties) in a hemispheric context; and different Latin American and Caribbean countries apparently prefer not to negotiate very much at all on a number of themes, such as intellectual property protection, foreign competition in government procurement, open trade in many services (such as telecommunications), and foreign investment practices.

Third, many tensions still exist between the United States and hemispheric countries—how far to go with respect to trade opening (as noted above) and hemispheric concern about U.S. direct and indirect protectionism (in agriculture, especially the use of domestic subsidies, and the promiscuous use of trade safeguard measures). U.S.-hemisphere tensions run quite deep at present over U.S. policy in Iraq, and more generically about what most LAC countries perceive to be growing U.S. unilateralism in foreign policy generally. This latter cause of tension affects Canada-U. S. relations as well as relations between the United States and LAC countries.

Fourth, much of the traditional tensions that have existed for a century or more persist, such as a hemispheric sense of U.S. neglect, coupled with dislike of U.S. interference in the region to serve its foreign policy objectives. Considerable U.S. condescension toward LAC countries manifests itself in derogatory and peremptory statements by government officials and members of Congress, as well as in such actions as insistence in the past on the useless exercise certifying whether LAC countries are cooperating sufficiently in fighting narcotraffic. There is much uncertainty in the region today about where the United States would come down if it proves impossible to both foster trade and combat terrorism.

The inability of LAC countries to cooperate among themselves is a source of weakness on their part in dealings with the United States. LAC countries, over the years, have shed many habits that had been ingrained over long periods. The shift from import-substituting development policy and discomfort over large levels of foreign direct investment have given way to an export-driven development model, accompanied by the desire to attract FDI. The Mexican decision to forge an economic alliance with the United States under NAFTA is almost taken for granted now, 10 years after the agreement went into effect, but the profound shift in thinking that this involved for Mexico is largely forgotten. Mexico, over a long period, had a policy of having no policy toward the United States on migration issues; today, this issue dominates much of the bilateral discussion.

But there are contentious habits that persist. Mexico continues to burden its development prospects by a highly nationalistic stance on energy, so much so that a country with large, untapped reserves of natural gas is now an importer and risks future electricity shortages.

Brazil's foreign policy still seems to be dominated by its hegemonic pretensions in South America, even when this prejudices its trade relations with the United States. The same point can be made concerning the United States: its combination of condescension and neglect of its own hemisphere militates against optimal political and economic relations.

One final observation emerges from the essays in this section. The LAC region is now dedicated to the form of democracy more than in any other recent period. I use the word "form" because there have been many instances of overthrowing popularly elected governments while preserving the semblance of democracy. Alberto Fujimori stole an election in Peru, but was later forced to flee the country for Japan only when other scandals emerged. President Fernando de la Rúa was largely pushed into resigning as the Argentine economy worsened, only to be succeeded by a succession of interim presidents until Néstor Kirchner was elected in 2003. President Jamil Mahuad was forced to resign in Ecuador because of pressure from a military-indigenous alliance, and the newly elected president, Lucio Gutiérrez had been active in exerting that pressure. Hugo Chávez, who himself attempted a coup d'état some years before he was elected president, used a technique of repetitive referenda to change the constitution and the makeup of Venezuela's governance structure—frustrating representative democracy by excessive personal democracy.

The presidents of two important South American countries, Fernando Henrique Cardoso of Brazil and Carlos Menem of Argentina, pushed successfully to amend their countries' respective constitutions to permit reelection to second terms—and included the authority for their own reelections in these changes.

The LAC region is far more sophisticated, economically and politically, than it was, say, 25 years ago. Major problems of underdevelopment continue to exist, however, socially, economically, and politically. The U.S. posture toward Latin America is variable, generally distant, sometimes embracing, and frequently fashioned as an afterthought, but at least U.S leaders probably now recognize how costly poverty and turmoil in the region can be for the United States. This was demonstrated by U.S. support during the past decade of financially beleaguered countries, namely, Mexico, Brazil, Uruguay, and Argentina—despite considerable domestic opposition to these actions.

30 BRAZIL-U.S. ECONOMIC RELATIONS[*]

Brazil, until a few years ago, hardly registered on the official U.S. radar screen. Few congressional delegations visited there. Its people speak Portuguese, hardly a world language for the U.S. population. Its large cities were better known in the United States for their *favelas* than for any sense of social justice. The natural beauty of Rio de Janeiro became less appreciated as the media and word of mouth reported the dangers of strolling on its lovely beaches. The capital, Brasilia, was thought of as an anodyne, artificial city built to house a bureaucracy rather than as a place for people to live. The military ran the country until the 1980s. Brazil was best known as a country of promise that was never realized.

There is another picture of Brazil that is now coming to the fore. Brazil is a vibrant democracy—almost too vibrant, in light of its contentious political parties. Its president, Fernando Henrique Cardoso, is probably the most admired head of government in the Americas in terms of intellect and personality. Brazil has a population of 170 million, or 49 percent of all of South America. Its gross domestic product is $765 billion, the second largest in the Americas after the United States and 36 percent of the GDP of all of Latin America and the Caribbean together.

Brazil's economy is the eighth largest in the world. Net annual foreign direct investment has been about $30 billion per year during the past two years. The only Latin American country that is even close is Mexico, where the comparable annual figure has been around $13 billion. U.S. merchandise exports to Mexico dwarf those to Brazil—$111 billion to $15 billion in 2000—but Brazil dominates U.S. exports to South America. It took the U.S. government a long time to pay attention to Brazil, but the private sector has not been as laggard.

This brief excursion into some data about Brazil is intended as a prelude for commenting on the tension that exists between the United States and Brazil about the path toward a Free Trade Area of the Americas. Official U.S. sources, sometimes directly but more often through off-the-record remarks, have been consistent in painting Brazil as a recalcitrant negotiator. Many members of the U.S. Congress and their

---

[*] *Issues in International Political Economy*, no. 16 (April 2001).

staffers make clear in private statements that Brazil is the most difficult country in the hemisphere in getting on with the free-trade negotiations. Their remarks have gone as far as saying that the United States should go ahead without Brazil, if necessary, to complete the FTAA negotiations, and allow Brazil to sign up later—and they seem to be confident that Brazil would do so.

Brazil, at times, has stimulated this contentiousness. In earlier years when the FTAA negotiations were just getting under way, Brazilian officials stated that the agreed 2005 date to complete the negotiations was an option, not a fixed target. President Cardoso of Brazil said recently that making Mercosul work is Brazil's destiny, whereas the FTAA is an option.[1] The two can coexist, and it is hard to understand why this comment was necessary other than to downplay the FTAA just before a meeting of heads of state intended to move the hemispheric free-trade process along. Brazil's import tariffs (really those of Mercosul, which, in theory, has a common external tariff) are relatively high, about 15 percent on average, and it was the unwillingness to consider lowering them in the near future that prompted Chile to give up on its negotiations to enter Mercosul and instead to reopen free-trade negotiations with the United States. In a comment that may have been more candid than he intended, a senior official of Itamaraty (the Foreign Ministry, which is responsible for Brazil's trade negotiations) said to a colleague and me that Brazil felt that it still had scope for import substitution industries. The translation to the uninitiated is that Brazil should keep many tariffs high for now to protect industries that may not otherwise be able to compete—the auto industry may be one example of this.

There have been endless interpretations of Brazil's position in the FTAA negotiations. The one most often heard is that Brazil wishes to remain the hegemon in South America, and the FTAA would undermine this position because of the power of the United States. Brazil's efforts to reach free-trade agreements between Mercosul and other South American countries gave some credence to this analysis. Another argument, one used by Brazil itself, is that while the United States wants all other countries to alter their import protection—even to change laws to accomplish this—the United States is not prepared to make concessions on issues of importance to the Latin American countries. What Brazil has mainly in mind in this assertion are the high U.S. price supports and import restrictions for agricultural products, such as sugar, peanuts, tobacco, and chocolate, which for the most part seem non-negotiable. The United States has also made clear that it is reluctant—that may not be a strong enough word—to revise its antidumping laws and procedures, which severely limit Brazil's exports of orange juice, steel, and shoes.

There is much justice in this Brazilian argument in that these restrictions do limit many of Brazil's most competitive exports. Brazilian spokesmen even put a number on the export loss from these restrictions—$10 billion a year. The figure may not be precise, but the argument is valid.

In a statement issued on April 7 by the 34 trade ministers of the hemisphere, the question of the date for concluding the FTAA negotiations was settled—no later than January 2005, allowing one year to complete the national ratification processes. The United States had been pushing for an earlier date, despite the knowledge that Brazil opposed this. The important point is that all the governments—Brazil included—have now signed on to this date.

There remain many deep problems in concluding the negotiations by the target date. These include tariff reductions, lowering impediments to trade in agriculture, devising rules for investment, working out rules of origin, and setting up a dispute-settlement mechanism. Before these substantive negotiations come into play, however, the U.S. president will have to secure trade promotion authority from the Congress, which would permit the final agreement to be dealt with as a package, no doubt with some modifications but not wholesale amendments. Absent this authority, many countries will not put forward their final offers if the final bargain has to be renegotiated with the U.S. Congress. Many members of Congress are insisting on trade and environmental conditions before granting trade promotion authority and are supporting the AFL-CIO position that if core labor standards and agreed environmental provisions are violated, the punishment should be import restrictions. Brazil fiercely opposes this, as do many other hemispheric countries. The elliptical language of the April 7 trade ministerial statement contains the following long sentence:

> We reiterate that one of our general objectives is to strive to make our trade liberalization and environmental policies mutually supportive, taking into account work undertaken by the World Trade Organization and other international organizations, and to further secure, in accordance with our respective laws and regulations, the observance and promotion of worker rights, renewing our commitment to the observance of

internationally recognized core labor standards, and acknowledging that the International Labor Organization is the competent body to set and deal with these labor standards.

To interpret: the International Labor Organization (ILO), and not bodies set up by the FTAA, will deal with these labor standards.

It serves no purpose to castigate Brazil for seeking to protect its interests—all countries do. It is sophistry to talk about an FTAA that excludes 36 percent of the economy of Latin America and the Caribbean. We must learn to get over our exclusive concentration on U.S. political limits, which ignores those of all other countries. We have an opportunity to unify the hemisphere in trade terms, and it would be a major loss if we squandered this.

Note

[1] Mercosul (Mercosur in Spanish) is the customs union among Brazil, Argentina, Paraguay, and Uruguay. The president's priority is understandable in that Mercosul has significant political content in the southern part of the hemisphere.

31 THE U.S.-CHILE CONNECTION*

Chile has long received outsized attention from U.S. authorities, sometimes beneficial, sometimes unfortunate. "Outsized" in that Chile is a country of only 15 million people, a long way from the United States, with a current GDP of $70 billion. To put this into context, the gross product of Washington, D.C., which has a population of about 525,000, is $55 billion. Eduardo Frei Montalva, Chile's president during the 1960s, once commented that if the long sliver of land that is his country slipped off into the Pacific, the rest of the world would barely notice.

When Frei was president, Chile was perhaps the country most favored in per capita resource receipts under the Alliance for Progress. When Salvador Allende was elected president in 1970, the U.S. government conspired with various Chilean conservative groups to prevent him from taking office. The United States was a staunch supporter of the Pinochet *golpe* in 1973 in which Allende was killed, and then it turned a blind eye to the horrible political excesses of the Pinochet regime. U.S. support was again vigorous when a majority of the Chilean population voted "no" in the plebiscite in 1988 and the country returned to democracy over the next two years. When NAFTA went into effect in 1994, the U.S. government told the Chileans that they were next. Maybe they will be (not as a party to NAFTA, but as the first country to have free-trade agreements with each of the three NAFTA members), but much time has passed since the first promise.

Why Chile, why always Chile, in good times and bad? There is no simple answer. Chile was an established democracy in the 1960s and this surely counted for something in those years. The Allende experience demonstrated that a country could democratically elect a Marxist president, but the U.S. government feared the precedent more than it favored democracy. When Chile restored democracy, this was supported vigorously by the United States—almost as though it wanted to make amends for U.S. behavior during the Pinochet years. The promise of NAFTA membership was based largely on the open and market-dominated economic policy of Chile, which was put into effect under

---

* *Issues in International Political Economy*, no. 18 (June 2001).

Pinochet and continued when the democratic *concertación* (the alliance between the Christian Democrats, Socialists, and some other parties) took office. Chile experimented with programs that were attractive to many Americans, such as privatization of social security, unilateral reduction of import barriers, and a uniform tariff. Chile was also exceedingly successful—its GDP grew by 7 percent a year from the mid-1980s to the late 1990s—and therefore was cited as an economic policy model for other Latin American countries.

U.S. attention to trade relations with Chile has persisted through Democratic and Republican administrations. The Clinton administration opened free-trade talks with Chile because of the conviction that an agreement would provide a stimulus for the wider negotiations for a Free Trade Area of the Americas. The argument was that if the U.S. Congress was presented with a concrete agreement, a favorable vote was more likely than for legislation as abstract as fast-track authority (i.e., legislation designed to deal with something that would be negotiated later). The Chileans were prepared to open negotiations with the United States because it had become evident that membership in Mercosur would require Chile to raise its external tariff and the Chileans were convinced that the main reason for their economic success was their open economy.

The Republicans who inherited the last-minute Clinton initiative also saw the Chilean free-trade negotiations as useful for their strategy. This, as articulated by Robert Zoellick, the U.S. trade representative, is to pursue the FTAA with vigor, but in the end sign agreements with any hemispheric countries prepared to do so. The Chileans fit the bill perfectly; they have said they are prepared to negotiate all issues as long as labor and environmental provisions, if they are violated, exclude the possibility of trade penalties. The bilateral negotiations are in full swing, indeed, at a frenzied pace, with the objective of having an approved agreement by the end of 2001. It is not yet clear how labor and the environment will be handled, or agriculture, or antidumping actions—all of which will be sensitive in the FTAA negotiations.

The U.S.-Chile negotiations are a gamble for both sides. If the negotiations fail, this could compromise the whole FTAA exercise. If they succeed—and my guess is that they will because the governments of both countries are making a determined effort that they do—this would stimulate proposals from other Latin America and Caribbean countries for free-trade area negotiations with the United States—

from Central America, the Caribbean, Colombia, and maybe even Argentina and Uruguay if a bilateral FTA with the United States has a higher probability of coming into existence than does the FTAA. If this were to occur, Mercosur would be destroyed.

If the Chile-U.S. FTA were to come into existence without fast-track authority (or trade-promotion authority, TPA, as it is now called), this would convince many in the Congress that TPA was not needed. TPA may not be needed for Chile, or for many other countries, but it is unlikely that Brazil would negotiate a trade agreement with the United States without TPA (i.e., with no limitation on congressional amendments). If congressional amendments gutted crucial elements of a negotiated FTA, the Chileans would then have to decide whether to walk away from the agreement or remove some of their own concessions. The Chileans seem prepared to take this risk.

Apart from how labor and the environment are handled, some difficult issues in the Chile-U.S. negotiations include agricultural restrictions on both sides, potential sensitivity on Chilean wine imports into the United States, and the U.S. use of antidumping duties. This last item was brought home to Chileans in late March this year, when the Growers League of Coachella Valley, California, filed a petition for antidumping duties of between 23 percent and 99.39 percent on Chilean grapes imported between April 1 and July 30, 2000. Table grapes are Chile's most important agricultural export to the United States; these imports from Chile in 1999 were $365 million. The U.S. International Trade Commission recently dismissed the dumping allegation, but the Chileans had to bear the cost of a legal defense. It was another example that fortified the deep conviction in Latin America that competitive success in the U.S. market will almost inexorably lead to antidumping charges, justified or not.

For the United States, an FTA with Chile is as much a precedent-setting matter as it is a trade-promoting exercise. This was also the case during all the years of failure to admit Chile into NAFTA. Chile refused to negotiate unless the U.S. president had fast-track authority and the U.S. government was unwilling to proceed unless the Congress granted fast track that embodied labor and environmental provisions that included trade sanctions. The issue then was not Chile; it was the broader issue of labor and environment punishment provisions for all negotiations. The issue now is less Chile per se than the demonstration that the United States can conclude trade agreements without fast track.

The FTA with Jordan went even further; it demonstrated that the United States was prepared to conclude a free *trade* agreement even if there is hardly any trade. The nub of the matter was to obtain labor and environmental provisions satisfactory to the Clinton administration. It remains unclear how the Bush administration will handle the Jordan agreement, other than to seek to refashion labor and environmental provisions in a way suitable to it.

Chile is not Jordan, but neither is it a major trading nation. U.S. exports to Chile in 2000 were about $3.5 billion, making it the fifth-largest market in the hemisphere (excluding Canada and Mexico, our NAFTA partners). Chile was the destination of 0.32 percent of all U.S. exports in 2000, and it supplied 0.22 percent of U.S. imports ($3.2 billion).[1]

Chile has shown that it is a remarkable country. It has gone through much in recent decades, from democracy under the elder Frei, to Marxism under Allende, to a form of fascism under Pinochet, and a return to democracy under President Patricio Aylwin. However, it is clear that President Frei was wrong—Chile is noticed, mostly in its own right, sometimes as an economic model for others to emulate or as a political model for others to avoid, and all too frequently for its value to establish precedents on a variety of issues of concern to the United States.

Note

[1] All data are from U.S. sources.

32 THE EVER-CHANGING U.S.-MEXICO RELATIONSHIP*

I have written extensively on U.S.-Mexican relations during the past several decades, perhaps more than on any other theme. I have a daughter who was born in Mexico and feel warmly toward the country. My research, visits, conversations, and analysis provide many insights—even if imperfect knowledge. Examination of this relationship became a national pastime last week when President Vicente Fox made a highly publicized state visit to the United States.

The overused cliché was that the United States had a love/hate attitude toward Mexico. This is too strong; the emotions never ran that deep. The duality of feeling was more like hope/disdain—a wish that Mexico would deal with its deep economic, social, and political problems, and at the same time an attitude of condescension that Mexico never seemed to accomplish this. The Mexican duality toward the United States was something on the order of ambiguity/mistrust—should Mexico embrace the United States or keep its distance out of wariness that it might be betrayed at crucial moments?

Fox, in his speech to a joint session of the U.S. Congress on September 6, said that the moment of change, particularly for Mexico, was when NAFTA came into existence, at the beginning of 1994. I agree with this judgment. NAFTA was the most profound agreement between the two countries in the twentieth century. NAFTA, in my view, used trade and investment as the route to long-term political embrace; and the extent to which this will go will be unknown for perhaps 50 years. I must confess that I had little sympathy with the NAFTA naysayers in either country because I felt that they lacked a sense of what neighborly relations could be—but instead focused on their particular interests or foibles, and not on how two countries thrown together by fate could and should handle their neighborly destinies. The obscenity of a rich United States coexisting with a poor neighbor is unhealthy for both, because it spawns such problems as undocumented migration, and is perpetually destabilizing.

The U.S. reception of Fox was remarkably warm. The Institutional Revolutionary Party (PRI) brought NAFTA into existence, but it was

---

* *Issues in International Political Economy*, no. 21 (September 2001).

Fox's victory in the July 2, 2000, presidential contest that alerted the U.S. audience that our neighbor to the south was transforming itself into a democracy. A troubled neighbor, an important economic partner, and a country that had shed much of its political authoritarianism—Fox embodied all these attributes.

Yet, considerable condescension toward Mexico remains in the U.S. body politic, as it does in popular sentiment. The congressional vote to prohibit Mexican trucks from crossing the border to deliver goods throughout the United States—despite a commitment to do so in an agreement approved by Congress—was an illustration of this. Domestic politics was more important to the U.S. Congress than the Mexican relationship, more important than keeping the United States' word. If, instead of Mexico, this had been a disagreement with Canada, or the United Kingdom, or Germany, would Congress have acted as it did? I doubt it. Will Congress give up its insistence on certifying Mexico's behavior in the fight against drug use? It has not until now, despite the evident futility and resentment caused by this practice. Maybe now it will. If so, chalk this up to Fox.

The central theme of Fox's speeches in the United States was "trust." Trust your neighbor, and he will return this sentiment. Punish your neighbor to force him to change his ways, and you will earn no trust in return—nor is he likely to change his ways. Fox is correct that this trust does not yet exist in full measure in either direction. The reason for this goes back to another cliché about the relationship—that it is asymmetric. Mexican analysts invoke asymmetry constantly. Economic asymmetry explains migration from Mexico to the United States; power asymmetry explains the fluctuating U.S. attention on Mexico; democratic asymmetry explains the differences in the administration of justice; historic asymmetry explains the mutual mistrust. One could continue endlessly; the asymmetry is real and it has consequences.

The United States is most comfortable in its relations with other developed countries, those that have reasonably comparable per capita incomes. Maybe some day Mexican incomes will approach those in the United States, but not for many years. The United States has close relationships with countries that share some of the burden of common defense. This is unlikely for Mexico. Achieving truly mature relations will require other accomplishments: more trade and investment; sustained economic growth in Mexico; a deepening of democracy; a reduction in Mexican corruption; an equitable system of justice; and an end to the need for Mexicans to emigrate, in violation of U.S. laws, to support themselves and their families. A superior/dependent situation does not permit a dialogue of equals.

The two countries' separate but intertwined histories have left a legacy of hang-ups on both sides. Historical experience explains much about Mexico's drive to retain its economic and political independence, and why it chose to remain distant from its powerful neighbor. This exercise in limited engagement was reciprocated in the United States; Mexico was seen as a troublesome neighbor, a poverty-ridden country that could not provide jobs for all of its people but instead had to rely on the escape valve of migration to the United States. It was not too many years ago that a best-selling book was entitled *Bordering on Chaos*.[1]

Fox did not initiate the changes taking place in Mexico. Many initiatives, in addition to NAFTA, preceded his election. Mexico had long had a policy of avoiding the discussion of migration issues with the United States, but then undertook a joint study of this subject under President Ernesto Zedillo that was published in 1998. The electoral laws that permitted Fox's election obviously had to be enacted beforehand. The conclusion that engagement with the United States was preferable to distancing it was made before Fox. Fox owes a deep debt of gratitude to Zedillo for relinquishing the leadership without a financial crisis, something that had eluded PRI presidents for some 30 years.

What the Mexican leadership concluded before Fox was that economic independence was a charade given the limited size of the Mexican domestic market and the inability in any event to escape the consequences of U.S. economic policies. I have long believed that the most important U.S. actions toward Mexico are taken without regard to their effects on Mexico—actions like raising and lowering the federal funds rate and managing the U.S. economy so as to achieve growth. It is the level of this growth that rejects or stimulates imports from Mexico. When NAFTA was negotiated, the Mexican assessment was that national cultural identity need not be sacrificed in the pursuit of economic development. Indeed, without this development, a majority of Mexicans would have been excluded from the bulk of the nation's rich cultural offerings.

The United States responded positively to the Salinas proposal for free trade under the first President Bush. Presidents Bill Clinton and now George W. Bush have pushed this engagement further. The laggard has been the U.S. Congress because of a variety of parochial interests and an inability to shed long-ingrained habits of disrespect for Mexico.

Fox will not achieve all he seeks immediately—especially on U.S. immigration policy. Maybe never, but I doubt this. What his visit demonstrates is that he came to power at a propitious time, found a sympathetic ear in the person of the U.S. president, and has moved the negotiating agenda forward. This is not the end game—that must occur internally in each of the two countries—but it is a giant leap.

Note

[1] Andres Oppenheimer, *Bordering on Chaos: Guerrillas, Stockbrokers, Politicians, and Mexico's Road to Prosperity* (Boston, Mass.: Little Brown, 1996).

33 REJECTING THE LESSONS OF EXPERIENCE[*]

The turmoil that Argentina is now going through is so costly for the majority of the Argentinean population that it demands some answers to the question, "Did it have to happen?" The same question arose when the Mexican financial structure imploded in 1994. My single word answer in both cases is, "No." In each case, the disaster followed a similar— although not identical—trajectory; and in each case the political and technical authorities made a bet that they could manage discredited practices. And, in each case, they failed, thereby visiting great suffering on their populations.

The precipitating event of the Argentine debacle was an overvalued and, ultimately, untenable exchange rate. The convertibility scheme adopted in 1991 was brilliant in its simplicity. By assuring the public that enough dollars were to be held in official reserves to cover the monetary base and thereby guarantee that pesos could be exchanged for dollars, on demand, even a skeptical public found the approach credible. Runaway inflation was stopped in its tracks. Overall economic growth rates soared, at least for a while. The technique was a variant of the Mexican experiment that began in 1987: using the exchange rate as the anchor to defeat inflation.

What "did in" the Argentine experiment was the appreciation of the U.S. dollar. This led, inevitably under one-to-one convertibility, to the appreciation of the Argentine peso, and despite the preaching of ideologues that it is immoral to alter an exchange rate, the price of a country's money—its exchange rate—does affect its exports and imports. On top of this, Brazil devalued its currency, the real, in 1999, and what Argentina faced was the appreciation of its currency while that of the country that took one-third of its exports depreciated. Argentina nevertheless retained the overvalued exchange rate and, in the process, further destroyed the country's competitive position. Inflation was kept in check, but the country has suffered economic downturn ever since.

This description omits other aspects of Argentina's economic, political, and social situation. These include relatively modest fiscal deficits (the public-sector borrowing requirement averaged about 2 percent of

---

[*] *Issues in International Political Economy*, no. 25 (January 2002).

GDP between 1991 and 1998, at the national and provincial levels combined); growing social inequality and poverty; too many feckless politicians who looked at government service as a source of enrichment; and reckless borrowing, public and private, domestic and foreign. Argentina met its debt obligations by more borrowing, but this was a large Ponzi scheme because the inability to earn enough foreign exchange from exports meant that the rigid one-to-one structure had to collapse, sooner or later.

Mexico, in 1987, adopted a form of price controls, under what was called a *pacto de solidaridad*, to lower its inflation. The *pacto*, or agreement, called for the private sector to limit price increases, labor to limit wage demands, and the government to control its expenditures. When the *pacto* started, Mexico devalued its currency sharply to leave room for appreciation of the peso in order to prevent devaluation from raising inflation. The *pactos* were kept in place, with annual modifications, from 1987 through 1994. The anchor for Mexico's anti-inflation policy was an increasingly overvalued peso. Inflation declined gradually, year after year, rather than abruptly as it did in Argentina after convertibility, but economic growth in Mexico in these years was modest.

As in Argentina, the Mexican political authorities (the president) and the technicians (the finance minister, with the cooperation of the head of the central bank) were unwilling to change the exchange-rate structure, a form of crawling peg. Instead, they took the risk that they could delay devaluation until some time in the future. There was general agreement that the Mexican peso was overvalued, and the way the authorities dealt with this in foreign borrowing was to issue short-term notes that had a dollar guarantee—the so-called *tesobonos*. This house of cards collapsed in December 1994, about three weeks after the previous president left office. The Mexican authorities gambled, and the population lost.

As in Argentina, there were other elements in the Mexican collapse. There were assassinations of political leaders during 1994; the U.S. Federal Reserve raised the federal funds rate six times during the year, seriously affecting Mexico; the government budget was kept in balance, but development banks were allowed to provide uncollected credit that amounted to some 3 percent of GDP; political corruption continued much as before; and foreign borrowing, on short terms and at dollar equivalents, rose sharply even as official reserves declined from capital flight and efforts to support the exchange rate. In the end, however, what did Mexico in was an overvalued exchange rate that was kept in place far too long.

In the case of Brazil, the scenario unfolded differently. The real plan was put in place in mid-1994 in an effort to reduce inflation without burdening economic growth. As in Mexico, in Brazil the stable exchange rate worked and inflation was reduced. Brazil weathered the tequila effect of December 1994, when the Mexican peso depreciated, without any sharp change in the real plan. However, Brazil was hit sharply by the aftereffects of the Russian debt default in 1998 because investors either had to cover positions or became nervous about keeping capital in Brazil given its precarious situation. In January 1999, Brazil devalued the real and took other corrective measures. Brazil did not have the turmoil that either Mexico or Argentina faced when they were forced to devalue under the most adverse circumstances. Brazil acted more quickly, before a deepening crisis made action exceedingly costly.

The currencies of Brazil and Mexico are both floating, and thus far the mechanism is working. Argentina has announced that it will allow its currency to float for domestic transactions but that it will be controlled for foreign trade. That is, Argentina will have a dual exchange-rate system, justified by the assertion that because the one-to-one structure was in effect for so long, the country needed six months for moving to a single, floating currency. Argentina's new president, Eduardo Duhalde, has also stated that the country's opening to imports has been a disaster and that trade policy will become more nationalistic (protectionist).

At this point, two comments. Dual exchange rates have a history of failure, especially by abetting corruption. Argentina has tried protectionism before, especially under Juan Perón, and it did little other than to increasingly impoverish the country. In the interest of Argentina's future, one can only hope that the dual exchange-rate system does not last very long and that the economic nationalism will not be too severe.

The deeper issue is to ask why government leaders pursue policies that have a history of failures. This is a task for psychologists, not economists, but I will give it a try.

- It is politically unpopular to devalue a currency; therefore, why not push off the unpleasantness for as long as possible? The suffering for doing this will come later, perhaps on someone else's watch.

- Memories are short—those of the politicians and technicians who repeat past mistakes, and those of the general public. In addition, memories often gild the past, forgetting that Latin America's poverty and inequality were created during periods of past protectionism.

- Intelligent leaders become wedded to policies they put in place and are often emotionally unable to change what they have been doing. Domingo Cavallo was fabulously successful as economics minister in Argentina in the early part of the 1990s and dismally incorrect in his actions when he returned in the De la Rúa government in the same position. In Mexico, in 1994, both President Salinas and Finance Minister Pedro Aspe were so adamant about not devaluing the peso that they excluded technicians from policy deliberations when they did not agree with this position.

It is understandable that many analysts and business leaders prefer fixed exchange rates. When things are going well, this provides a degree of certainty. However, the time to judge the effectiveness of an exchange-rate mechanism is when the system is under pressure. This explains the attractiveness of floating exchange rates for countries prone to economic shocks. It is clear from what is happening in Argentina and what took place in Mexico in 1994 that fixed rates—even a relatively hard fix of the type that Argentina had—can spell disaster when a country is under economic pressure. Perhaps this lesson will stick—at least for a time.

34 MEXICO: LATIN AMERICA'S UNCERTAIN BRIGHT SPOT*

The three major economic rating agencies have accorded investment grade status to Mexican government obligations, thereby making this paper eligible for inclusion in many pension funds. The ratings are a testament to Mexico's solid macroeconomic management. When projected revenue declines, Francisco Gil-Díaz, the finance minister, does not hesitate to cut budgeted expenditures. In recent years, the Mexican peso has appreciated against the dollar—which, in large part, is a reflection of the conservative management of monetary policy by the Bank of Mexico. The ratings from Standard & Poor's, Moody's, and Fitch, however, are based more on a snapshot—the macroeconomic solidity of the moment—than a sophisticated analysis of the future.

By most reckonings, 2001 was not a good year for Mexico. Gross domestic product, which had grown solidly for the previous five years (i.e., after recovery from the disastrous economic decline in 1995), fell in 2001 by 0.3 percent. The main reason for the decline was the drop in exports to the United States, which had its own economic slowdown. The United States is the destination for 85 to 90 percent of Mexico's exports. This, however, was not the only reason for export problems. Industrial productivity declined in most sectors last year and unit labor costs rose. The high value of the peso in relation to the dollar was surely a drag on exports. GDP growth is expected to grow this year by only about 1 percent.

If these were the only economic indicators, a dynamic analysis might lead to the judgment that the problems of 2001 were merely a temporary hiatus in Mexico's successful march to a more prosperous future. Foreign direct investment is holding up (the total in 2001 was $25 billion, which includes the CitiBank purchase of Banamex), which implies that long-term investors have reached this conclusion. Other features must be taken into account, however. Perhaps the most important is that Mexico's export growth rate of some 20 percent a year in recent years is unlikely to be sustained in the future, particularly if the United States does not grow as rapidly as it did in the halcyon years of the later

---

* *Issues in International Political Economy*, no. 27 (March 2002).

1990s. Ever-growing exports to the United States in those years were the main engine for Mexico's economic growth, but this engine is likely to slow.

There were other disappointing developments in Mexico last year. The tax reform proposed by the government—whose central feature was to raise the value-added tax on food and medicines to 15 percent, thereby making the VAT rate uniform—failed miserably. Some reform was achieved in the income tax, but this was counterbalanced by a complicated luxury tax that most Mexican economic analysts hope can be discarded quickly. Other structural reforms have gone nowhere. These include making the labor market more flexible, simplifying investment in electricity generation, opening natural gas exploration to private investors, reforming the telecommunications structure, and altering the judicial system, especially as it applies to mercantile law. The electricity rate structure for consumers was altered in early 2002 and this change raised the cost to middle-class ratepayers by 25 to 50 percent.

Mexico's net domestic savings rate remains low, in the neighborhood of 17 percent, and tax collections as a percent of GDP are about 11 to 12 percent, low even by Latin American standards. This throws a heavy burden on Pemex, which picks up much of the revenue shortfall, thereby shortchanging its ability to invest in oil and gas exploration and exploitation. Because Pemex is the only source for investment in the oil industry in Mexico, this translates into inadequate investment in this vital sector.

Polls indicate that the popularity of President Vicente Fox is declining steadily; it is now below 50 percent and seems to slide further in each successive poll. The economy is in the doldrums, and this diminishes the president's popularity.

Many Mexicans lost jobs last year and, in addition, there was a 300,000-person shortfall in job creation for the one million new entrants in the labor force. Fox and his team were seen as inept negotiators with the legislature on taxes and the budget. Democracy, including an independent legislature dominated by the opposition, is a relatively new phenomenon in Mexico, and the political class is still learning how to deal with this.

Some of the problems of 2001 and early 2002 may be manageable in the months and years ahead. The Institutional Revolutionary Party has just chosen a new leader, Roberto Madrazo, and he may show a willingness to negotiate structural issues with the government. The peso, which is probably overvalued, may decline in value during the coming months; the peso is not being propped up by active intervention or high interest rates. Mexico needs considerable investment in infrastructure, and funds for this should be available from the international development institutions. The learning curve for dealing with an opposition-led legislature may speed up.

Other issues, however, require more complex solutions. These include the main structural impediments to growth, raising the low savings rate and thereby reducing the large reliance on capital inflows, and dealing with the growing lawlessness in many Mexican cities. Efforts to deal with these matters have not succeeded in the past, including when the PRI ran both the executive and the legislature. The capacity to deal with these structural issues is really at the heart of Mexico's economic future. If the export engine is slowing, supplementary measures are needed.

The mood in Mexico is one of disillusion. President Fox is not meeting the expectations aroused by candidate Fox. The problems are not necessarily his entire making, but his watch is a historic one after 71 years of PRI domination. This mood of disappointment, especially from middle-class voters who supported Fox, was the dominant impression I took away after a recent visit to Mexico. Mexico has a solid macroeconomic foundation, and this impresses Wall Street and foreign investors, but makes little impression on those Mexicans who expected more tangible progress under a new, non-PRI administration.

The year 2001 was only the first of a six-year term, and there is plenty of time to turn around negative impressions. A U.S. recovery, even if modest, will help, and a sustained U.S. recovery will help even more. A less confrontational atmosphere between the congress and the presidency would help alter the mood of helplessness, which informed Mexicans now take for granted when it comes to innovation in public affairs. Fox's cabinet, which has been replete with internal quarrels, does not have a good reputation in Mexico and some changes will probably occur—although not in the economic sphere. What is needed most of all, however, are structural reforms that will convince Mexicans and foreigners alike that Mexico is prepared to confront its problems head on. The nature of these reforms has already been cited.

What role can the United States have in helping to turn around what I found to be a pessimistic mood in Mexico? The most important action is to run the U.S. economy well because the growth in U.S. GDP is the key determinant of Mexico's exports. In this respect, keeping one number in mind is useful: exports to the United States make up 30 percent of Mexico's GDP.

The two countries (three, if Canada is included) are in the ninth year of an integration process that has come a long way since NAFTA was first proposed, and the relationship has been transformed beyond anyone's expectations a decade ago. The integration process still has a long way to go, however—in facilitating trade, promoting investment, intensifying official and informal contacts, and stimulating knowledge of each other's cultures. Bringing the two countries even closer in the years ahead requires a prosperous and self-confident Mexico, and not a country that looks to its neighbor to the north as an escape valve for its impoverished population. This kind of economic advance will not come without structural changes—and these are needed sooner rather than later if the Fox administration is to be a successful one.

35 UNCERTAINTY IN VENEZUELA*

Note: After the following essay was written, the situation in Venezuela changed abruptly and Hugo Chávez returned to power as president of Venezuela. It is too soon to predict the implications of this series of events on Venezuela's internal and foreign policy.

Hugo Chávez was forced to resign as president of Venezuela on April 11, 2002. He took office in February 1999 and, therefore, was president for about 39 months. The defined term for the presidency in the new constitution—Chávez' constitution—is six years. His period in the presidency was tempestuous, and made fundamental changes in Venezuela's institutional structure.

These monthly notes focus primarily on economic matters, but the political context is essential in dealing with issues of "political economy." Chávez won the presidency—two times, in fact, first in normal fashion and them again a short time later after the new constitution was promulgated—with overwhelming majorities. His coattails at the outset were long enough for him to have large majorities in the unicameral legislature. He was able as well to stack the judiciary. Over time, though, Chávez managed to alienate most key groups in Venezuelan society, including business, labor, the church, and university communities. Even though he came out of the military, Chávez also managed to turn the military against him and, in the end, this proved fatal to his administration. It became clear as time passed that Chávez had the ability to overturn the inadequate social and economic structure of Venezuela that preceded him, but he lacked the talent and temperament to run a country.

Chávez' shortcomings showed up emphatically in the economic sphere. For Venezuela watchers, both inside and outside the country, it was never clear that Chávez had a stated economic policy, and surely not a coherent one. The history of modern Venezuela is that the country prospered when oil prices were high and stagnated when they were low. Oil exports were 80 percent of the total, more or less year in and year out, and little was done to diversify the economy to smooth out the booms and busts. Until Chávez, the country was unable even to set up an emergency fund to tide it over the inevitable bad times.

---

* *Issues in International Political Economy*, no. 28 (April 2002).

The political structure that dominated pre-Chávez Venezuela consisted of two main parties, both of which lost prestige during several decades, a reality that facilitated Chávez' ascent to power. Now that Chávez is gone and an interim civilian president is in place, a new political structure will have to be fashioned. Maybe even a new constitution. How this is done will be a critical issue for the future.

Beyond that, and moving to economics, inequalities in Venezuela are great and poverty is high. I do not fully believe that the 70 percent figure that is thrown around regularly is accurate, but I do not doubt the reality that a majority of Venezuelans live in poverty. Chávez played heavily on the dismal social situation in Venezuela to achieve power. Venezuela has long had a history of low tax collections, which hardly bespeaks much concern on the part of the dominant economic class.

The difficulties that Chávez faced built up gradually during the course of his presidency. Oil is at the heart of the Venezuelan economy, and it is fitting that the precipitating event that led to Chávez' ouster (more formally, his resignation) also had to do with oil. The one Venezuelan institution that was respected for its probity and efficiency was Petroleos de Venezuela, S.A. (Pedevesa) and, from the outset, Chávez tried to politicize this institution. Its respected president was forced out. A succession of military officers was appointed to run Pedevesa and then, more recently, five new members were proposed for the board of directors. It was not apparent that they were qualified for the positions, but Chávez obviously felt they would be loyal to him. The career employees and managers of Pedevesa protested. They called a one-day strike on April 9, and other labor and business groups joined them. The work stoppage was so successful that its organizers decided to continue the action for a second day, and then indefinitely. On the third day, April 11, hundreds of thousands of demonstrators marched on the presidential palace. Chávez was defiant, tried to organize a counter-demonstration, and cut off television coverage of the protest, and a number of protestors were killed by gunfire. The military stepped in, ostensibly to keep order, and that was that for Chávez.

It is now time to look ahead. There is no innate reason why the Venezuelan economy cannot be restored to healthy growth—the oil is there, as is the market—but the status quo ante may no longer be acceptable to the general population. Chávez was chosen president because the old system had fallen into disrepair. The various societal groups worked together to oust Chávez, but the task now is more complex—to work together to fashion a more just economic structure. As one looks to the future, the challenges are daunting: Will corruption be challenged head on? Will wealthy Venezuelans pay their taxes? Will an effort be made to diversify economic production? Will there be a serious effort to reduce poverty? All of these problems must be addressed despite the lack of respected political leaders.

There are related political issues. The final arbiter to sack Chávez was the military. To a large extent, the military has long played this role in Venezuela. What does this say about the vigor of Venezuela's democracy? The leaders of the street demonstrations surely were cognizant that President Fernando De la Rúa of Argentina was forced to resign following large street demonstrations. The former president of Ecuador, Jamil Muhuad, was forced out earlier in similar fashion. President Alberto Fujimori of Peru stole an election, but was forced out of office as scandal was budding. Hemispheric leaders have now made democracy a sine qua non of political practice in their countries. Is it democratic to oust leaders by means of street demonstrations? In any event, this is apparently acceptable if one makes allowances for the sponginess of Latin American democracy, as long as the military makes no effort to run the country afterward.

How will the developments in Venezuela be perceived elsewhere in Latin America and in the United States? Ambiguously, I am sure. Leaders in some other Latin American countries are likely to think, "There but for the grace of God (or circumstances), go I." On the other hand, Chávez was troublesome for other Latin American leaders, and most will not be unhappy to see him gone. Had the ouster been organized by elements of the U.S. government, this would have elicited outrage—but the evidence is that Venezuelans instigated Chávez' removal.

As to U.S. policy, the first reaction will be to allow "the dust to settle." It is not clearly known how many protestors were killed, or by whom, or how Venezuelans will now organize their political and economic structure. No tears will be shed in the U.S. government, or by U.S. business leaders, over the ouster of Chávez. Just the reverse, in fact. If the military tries to openly retain power, this will lead to U.S. government criticism, but the Venezuelan military surely understands this. If the oil flows again, President Bush's administration will surely be satisfied. If I were to give advice to the U.S. government, it would be to allow what comes next to be a Venezuelan show—at least, publicly. Large financial support should not be needed, and this eases U.S. policy decisions.

The U.S. Congress and the public at large are likely to react somewhat disdainfully—after all, these things are common in Latin America. Unfortunately, they are. Yet there is no country named "Latin America." The big countries, Brazil and Mexico, have functioning political systems. So does Chile. The analysis must be made country by country—and Venezuela was a country ripe for this kind of change.

Where should Venezuela be going in the longer term? The answer, I believe, is that the leaders must be more constructive than in the recent past. If the country fails to diversify, it dooms itself to a seesaw economic future with the ups and downs of oil prices. If the leaders fail to address corruption, the new government will fall into the same disrepute that prevailed before and during the Chávez period. If poverty is not addressed, there is little reason for the majority of the population to support the new government. If social concerns are ignored, trouble will be brewed for the future.

The tasks ahead are reasonably clear conceptually, but damnably complex in practice. Will Venezuela find leaders up to the task ahead? One surely hopes so.

36 THE BRAZIL-U.S. RELATIONSHIP: A TALE OF MUTUAL IGNORANCE*

One variant of Murphy's Law is that when matters get dicey in one aspect of a country's affairs, they get tense across the board. This is happening this year in Brazil. The long-running troubles in Argentina became critical early in the year and the repercussions inevitably spill over the border into Brazil, both politically and economically. Luiz Inácio "Lula" da Silva of the Workers Party (PT) ran up a commanding lead in the polls for the presidential election scheduled for October, and the concern this generated in world money markets led to an increase earlier this month in the spread of Brazil's sovereign bonds (the so-called sovereign risk) to more than 1,100 basis points over U.S. Treasuries; the Brazilian real continued to slide against the dollar; and the difficulty in selling Brazilian treasury bills forced the central bank to issue short-duration bills, exacerbating the country's already unsatisfactory debt-maturity profile. Moody's Investors' Service changed its outlook on Brazil's foreign and domestic debt from positive to stable, noting that conditions for its debt rollover needs might not be favorable when these transactions have to take place.

Despite these problems, the Brazilian situation is by no means bleak, certainly not in comparison with other large Latin American countries—namely, Argentina, Colombia, and Venezuela. Brazil is likely to have positive GDP growth this year, but not much (perhaps as high as 2 percent, and therefore very little growth on a per capita basis). The country is meeting its fiscal target of a primary surplus of 3.5 percent of GDP. (The primary surplus omits interest payments and is targeted in order to prevent further debt buildup.) About 80 percent of Brazil's public sector debt is internal, and this stands in sharp contrast to the unmanageable public debt in Argentina, which is largely in U.S. dollars. Inflation in Brazil is still too high, but not inordinately so at about 7 to 8 percent on an annual basis in recent months compared with an annual goal of 6 percent. Foreign direct investment (FDI) into Brazil in 2002 is not keeping up with the torrid pace of recent years (about $25 billion a year), but should still be between $15 and $18 billion this year, making it second only to China among developing countries.

---

* *Issues in International Political Economy*, no. 30 (June 2002).

The FDI data highlight an anomalous situation, at least in terms of Brazil-U.S. relations. The United States is the leading country for foreign investment in Brazil, accounting for some 25 percent of the total. The U.S. private sector discovered the promise of Brazil many years ago and is making a big bet on the country's successful future. Much of the investment in the past was designed to exploit the domestic market, but increasingly it is intended as well to use Brazil as an export platform. The U.S. government and the U.S. Congress, by contrast, have been much slower to grasp the critical political-economic role of Brazil in South America. They took 18 months to replace the last ambassador, a reality that can best be described as scandalous. U.S. officials have been sniping regularly at Brazil during the last few years as holding back progress on establishing the Free Trade Area of the Americas, whereas in reality the United States has done more to slow progress in this hemispheric endeavor, particularly by the failure of Congress to grant fast-track trade negotiation authority to two successive presidents.

Brazilian officials are quick to point out that U.S. import restrictions against Brazilian exports are significant, targeting in particular agricultural products. On top of this existing grievance, the U.S. Congress recently passed a farm bill that sharply increases U.S. income support to growers, thereby threatening Brazilian exports, especially soybeans, not only in the U.S. market but also in third markets. President Bush signed this bill, so the blame cannot be placed solely on Congress. The conclusion of most Brazilians, as I discovered on a recent trip, is that the U.S. government does not care—and that it does not even want to hear what the Brazilian authorities are saying.

However deserved the criticism is about U.S. negligence, most Brazilian problems—political and economic—are created in Brazil. Brazil is not a major trading nation. Its exports are only about 10 percent of GDP. (For comparison, Mexico's exports are about 35 percent of GDP.) Brazil's current account deficit in recent years has been averaging around 4.5 percent of GDP, clearly on the high side. This, plus debt amortizations, translate into a need for external financing this year of more than $50 billion, which helps explains the recent downgrading by Moody's of Brazil's debt outlook. If Brazil is unable to deal with its balance-of-payments problem by increasing its export earnings, the country will remain vulnerable to any shock that reduces the inflow of foreign capital.

Concern about a Lula victory in the presidential election is part of the vulnerability that Brazil faces in its external sector. Lula has changed his rhetoric this time from what it was in his previous three presidential campaigns. He does not advocate debt restructuring. He is not adamantly adverse to trade negotiations. When he reverts to past populism, his statements are quickly reinterpreted. Many money market observers of Brazil have elephantine memories, however, and they remember Lula's past pronouncements. In addition, there is no evidence that his closest advisers have changed their outlooks. Hence, the nervousness. Lula has high polling numbers, especially in comparison with José Serra, the candidate of the current government coalition (more than 40 percent for Lula and around 20 percent for Serra as this is written), but the undecided numbers are high. Lula has been at this level before at this stage of previous campaigns and still lost. Yet, this may be the time when the high early numbers stick. The campaign will not get going in earnest until the World Cup in soccer is completed.

The Brazilian scene should be put in context by understanding Brazil's role in Latin America and the country's salience in terms of U.S. policy toward the hemisphere. Brazil is the dominant country in South America in population (172 million of South America's 350 million) and economic size. It is also the one country in South America with a sophisticated industrial structure in a number of important sectors. When the United States took action to restrict steel imports, Brazil was the country most affected in South America. Brazil, in other words, is a country that must be reckoned with if the United States is to have a meaningful hemispheric policy.

Trade—or the trade-investment combination—is the critical issue in Brazil-U.S. relations, just as it is in U.S. policy toward Latin America as a whole. This reality is what makes the U.S. farm bill— which, if it remains in place, will have a severe adverse effect on Brazil's exports and, hence, on the country's pace of economic growth—such a devastating action. In my recent visit, the common refrain was that it is naïve to listen to the words of U.S. leaders on "free" trade; it is much more important to look at what the United States does (impose import restrictions to satisfy domestic political constituencies) or does not do (in the case of the Congress, provide meaningful trade-negotiation authority).

Consummation of the FTAA is in some doubt because of the combination of uncertain or potentially restrictive fast-track action and growing U.S. protectionism. And just as it will be difficult to have a positive relationship with Brazil in the absence of mutually beneficial trade policy, so will it be impossible to have a productive relationship with Latin America as a whole without an open U.S. market. Failing that, none of the other U.S. initiatives—promoting democracy, combating corruption, and seeking cooperation on anti-terrorism—hold much promise. The primary objective of Latin American countries is the achievement of high growth rates and this, given their export orientation, requires an open U.S. market.

It has become clear during the past several years that neither the United States nor Brazil knows the other country very well—what their deep aspirations are, how their domestic politics work, how they make decisions—and this is a serious deficiency. Brazilians undoubtedly know more about the United States than the reverse. We have learned repeatedly in recent years that the price of ignorance can be high—Afghanistan is the most recent example, but by no means the only one. It is unconscionable that this ignorance should exist in the United States about the most important country in South America—a region that we consider to be in our neighborhood.

37 THE UNITED STATES AND LATIN AMERICA: MUTUAL DISAPPOINTMENTS*

Latin America has become a metaphor for U.S. neglect interrupted by spasms of crisis-driven attention. U.S. presidential candidates talk up the region, only to pay it little heed once elected. George Bush's attention to the region, Mexico mostly, lasted longer than that of many of his predecessors, but then the routine inattention set in after September 11, 2001. The best example of presidential scorn is the one that Sol Linowitz related: Lyndon Johnson asked him on the airplane to a hemispheric summit conference in Punta del Este why he was going to Uruguay at all. The one context in which an indirect focus on Latin America has grown is electoral, to get the votes of *Latinos* living in critical U.S. states like California, Texas, and Florida.

The Latin American counterpart to U.S. neglect and crisis-driven attention is distrust. The hemispheric countries south of the United States do not have the luxury of ignoring their powerful northern neighbor, to which they send about 40 percent of their exports (80 to 85 percent for Mexico) and from which they receive from one-half to two-thirds of their foreign investment. But Latin American intellectuals do not hesitate to show their disdain for U.S. promises not kept, protection that keeps out their goods, attacks that target their failures to stem drug trade, and lectures on the virtues of market disciplines even as these break down in the United States. It was no surprise to hemisphere watchers that majorities of the population in most Latin countries, especially the big ones like Brazil and Mexico, did not want to become too entangled in the U.S. anti-terrorism campaign after 9/11. Nor was it any surprise to watchers in Latin America that U.S. attention would turn elsewhere.

U.S. disappointments with Latin America are many. Democracy did not take root in the region until recently, and even now it is shaky in country after country. Economic development has lagged, certainly as compared with Asia. The Latin American region has a more unequal income distribution than any other region of the world, and this is not just an artifact of "neoliberalism." Poverty is rampant. It is only today

---

* *Issues in International Political Economy*, no. 32 (August 2002).

that educational opportunity is opening widely. The word "disappoint-ments" was used because the dominant culture in Latin America is Eu-ropean, just as in North America. The cultural legacy, however, obviously took a different turn from that of North America.

Latin American disappointments with its own performance took the form of blaming others over many decades. At one point, the dominant philosophical outlook of Latin American thinkers was "dependency." Latin America was part of the periphery and the United States and oth-er developed countries were the center, and the periphery did not make great economic strides because of the behavior of the center. The depen-dency theory had no echo in Asia, where growth was consistently high-er than in Latin America. Latin American development thinkers were export pessimists; their reasoning was that to the extent that merchan-dise exports succeeded in penetrating the markets of the center, action would be taken to cut off those exports. Japan, Korea, Thailand, and oth-er Asian countries looked to exports to drive their development rather than think in pessimistic terms. Other words are used today to blame others—such as the neoliberal development model allegedly foisted on them. Yet, the internal exploitation of populations long antedated these explanations. For all its talented people, Latin America still struggles with underdevelopment. Some years ago a Mexican intellectual asked me: "Do you think that Mexico will ever become a developed country?" I answered, "Yes." But the process is interminable.

The disappointments move in the other direction as well. Americans have deplored the persistence of military governments that seized pow-er in Latin American countries, but they forget the role the United States played in supporting many of these. When Latin American countries elected leaders disliked by the U.S. government, there was lit-tle hesitancy to overthrow them. Export pessimism was a fact of life for many decades, but so was U.S. protectionism against the region's most competitive exports. U.S. politicians who fight to keep out goods com-ing from developing countries are protecting their constituents, but at the expense of jobs elsewhere. The U.S. Congress shows little hesitancy in heavily subsidizing agricultural production without much regard to how this affects farmers in Latin America. The United States insists on passing judgment as to whether other countries are cooperating in the campaign against narcotrafficking with little thought given to the reality that others are implicitly passing judgment on the efficacy of the U.S. measures to fight drug use.

Paul O'Neill, the U.S. treasury secretary, told Fox News a few weeks ago that he saw no reason to offer financial support at this time to Brazil and other Latin American countries, that what was needed were homegrown policies that do some good and not funds "that just go out of the country to Swiss bank accounts." Then, a week or so later, a U.S. loan of $1.5 billion was provided to Uruguay as a bridge until an IMF program goes into effect, and the United States supported a $30 billion IMF support package to Brazil. Did the angry reaction to Secretary O'Neill's Swiss bank account comment influence the shift in U.S. policy? My guess is that it did, to some extent.

Hate is not the right sentiment to describe relations between the United States and Latin America, or between the people of the two regions. The mutual feelings are more nuanced than that. The United States, its government and probably a majority of its population, looks down on Latin America and sees it as a region that cannot get its act together. Denigration of this sort leads to neglect. There have been periods when U.S. leaders tried to overcome this bias—and met with temporary success. The Good Neighbor Policy under Franklin D. Roosevelt and the Alliance for Progress under John F. Kennedy were examples of these efforts. In due course, however, the normal pattern of neglect returned.

The majority of Latin Americans have a high regard for the open U.S. political system and the success of the U.S. economy. There is some natural antipathy toward the rich hegemon, but no more so than exists elsewhere. What does grate, however, is the hypocrisy that is perceived—lectures that are ill informed, promises that are not kept, and actions that display contempt.

To a policy wonk, the natural question that arises is: What can be done to alter attitudes and behavior? I doubt that the answer is a better propaganda office operating out of the White House. On the substantive side, the most important U.S. action would be to get on with the negotiation and establishment of the Free Trade Area of the Americas. Latin American development policy is predicated on export expansion, and if U.S. policy narrows this opportunity, no amount of verbiage can correct this. Fortunately, a major positive step in this direction has just been taken with passage of trade promotion authority, but the eventual proof will be in the negotiation and congressional approval of what comes out of that.

Officials must be careful with their words. The administration, in effect, apologized for Secretary O'Neill's derogatory comment, but this does not remove the inner annoyance of Brazilian and other Latin leaders. When congresspeople make nasty comments, as they often do, the administration should openly make its disagreement known. Most Latin Americans do not distinguish sharply between the administration and the Congress. For months, in connection with the preliminary discussions on the FTAA, snide anti-Brazilian comments were leaked in an attempt to override Brazilian resistance to some U.S. proposals. Such behavior is unworthy, especially when dealing with such an important country.

There must be no ambiguity as to the U.S. position in support of democracy. The uncertainty about the U.S. position at the time of the aborted coup in Venezuela in April of this year was exceedingly damaging. The July report of the inspector general that spells out that the behavior of the State Department was supportive of democracy in Venezuela should be made public in order to dispel the widespread contrary impression.

Latin American issues do not deal with war and peace, as do those relating to the Middle East, Northeast Asia, and South Asia. Argentina and Brazil gave up their nuclear arms pretensions, and this simultaneously eased U.S. problems and fostered U.S. neglect of the region. If the United States engages substantively with Latin America, particularly in the trade arena, this will do much to change regional attitudes as well. Failing that, the painful and damaging mutual sniping will continue.

38 CHILE AS A TEMPLATE*

Latin America and the Caribbean went through two successive dreadful economic decades, the 1980s and 1990s, and the horror is continuing in the first two years of this century. The political situation has been much better, in that authoritarian and military regimes were discarded in favor of democracies even during the worst economic years of the 1980s and democracy continues to this day as the most favored form of government. These are tarnished democracies in some cases, but there has been no the reversion to the military takeovers that pessimists regularly predict when the situation in many countries looks particularly terrible. However, horrible economic outcomes have their political consequences, as we are seeing in one election after another in the region.

As observers of the Latin American scene know, the major exception to the economic catastrophe that dominated the regional scene over the past two decades was Chile. The positive economic performance of Chile compared with the rest of the region is shown in figure 1. A few other countries have had considerable growth in the 1990s—Costa Rica, El Salvador, the Dominican Republic, Trinidad and Tobago, and Mexico—but none as consistently as Chile over the full 1985 to 2000 period.

It is important to understand the policies that made Chilean economic performance unique in Latin America. Chile suffered through an economic collapse in 1982. The response, however, was not to jettison the liberal economic philosophy that had been put in place a decade earlier by the Pinochet regime, but rather to modify and even strengthen it. By liberal, I have in mind fiscal prudence, consistent monetary policy that aims at keeping inflation low, an exchange rate that is now cleanly floating, significant privatization of government enterprises, an open import market, encouragement of exports (which now make up 43 percent of GDP), targeted social programs during the difficult years, and a respected judicial system. Due mainly to its steady growth year after year, Chile reduced its poverty rate from 45 percent of the population in 1985 to 21 percent in 2000. The economic reforms were originally put in place by a dictatorial regime, but the policies

---

* *Issues in International Political Economy*, no. 35 (November 2002).

then continued, with some changes at the margin, when democracy was restored to Chile in 1990.

Figure 1. GDP Growth in Chile and LAC, 1985–2000 (annual in percent)

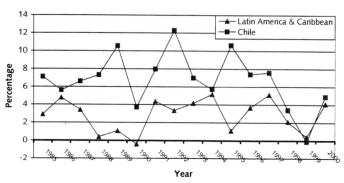

Source: *World Development Indicators* (Washington, D.C.: World Bank, 2002).

In the last few years, Chile's economic performance has been less stellar than earlier. There was actually a slight downturn in 1999, due perhaps to playing it ultrasafe by tightening monetary policy after the Asian crisis, and GDP growth this year is likely to be about 2 percent— not bad in the Latin American context, but a far cry from the consistent 7 to 8 percent growth performances of the heyday years. Much of the current problem can be attributed to the serious deterioration in the terms of trade represented by the low prices for copper exports (which still account for about 40 percent of Chile's total merchandise exports) and the high prices for oil imports. The business community is restive about the economic leadership being provided by President Ricardo Lagos, and the president is reacting to this. When I was in Chile a few weeks ago, Lagos said he would consider a pro-growth plan to institute a number of microeconomic stimuli suggested two years earlier by the Sociedad de Fomento Fabril (SFF), the large industrial organization of the private sector, but the acceptance was greeted with considerable cynicism. It came on the eve of the large annual dinner of the influential SFF at which President Lagos was to be the main speaker. Chile's electorate is fairly evenly divided between conservative parties and the *concertación* (or alliance) of Christian Democrats, Socialists, and other parties that have won the presidency in each of the three elections after democracy was restored. Lagos is a Socialist.

The larger context in which to analyze the Chilean scene is how its economic performance is likely to affect decisions of much of the rest of the region. Chile has succeeded with a liberal economic policy, while most of the rest of Latin America is failing with less rigorous adherence to liberal economic policies. Argentina ran fiscal deficits that were excessive for maintaining its fixed exchange rate; Brazil has contracted a dangerously high level of debt; Mexico used its exchange rate as the anchor to control inflation, which came unstuck in 1994; Venezuela put its trust in the hands of a president with little sense of economic fundamentals. The argument that globalism necessarily prejudices the development aspirations of developing countries is clearly contradicted by the Chilean performance; Chile globalized by passionately seeking foreign investment and promoting exports and succeeded in both, even as it outstripped the rest of the hemisphere in its economic growth.

If the Chilean model falters now, however, this pesky (to globalization opponents) pro-globalization success will lose much force. Latin Americans have pronounced the "Washington consensus" as dead for many years now, but there was Chile adopting most of the policy elements of the consensus and doing splendidly. Luis Inacio "Lula" da Silva won the recent election by calling for changes in the Brazilian economic model. Lucio Gutierrez, who emerged politically as an antimarket leftist, is now favored to win the presidency in the runoff in Ecuador. Evo Morales ran against the liberal economic model and came close to becoming the president of Bolivia. Hugo Chávez became president of Venezuela even as he expressed admiration for the Fidel Castro model in Cuba.

All these people stated a desire to do away with the liberal economic model, although they have been imprecise as to what their alternative would be. What they have argued is that the economic situation of the majority of the population in each of their countries has worsened under the liberal (they would use the word "neoliberal") development model, and therefore "it is time for a change." This is a potent argument because the situation of a majority of the population has stagnated.

The United States has been the most vociferous advocate of liberal economic policies. This was true under President Clinton and is even moreso now under President Bush. The proposal for a Free Trade Area of the Americas is predicated on liberal trade policies. Chile's success in forcing most of its producers to compete with imports and to exploit Chile's geography and assets in penetrating export markets has made its policies far more influential than its relatively small population would warrant.

If Chile's economy continues to falter, the consequences could be considerable throughout the hemisphere. In Chile itself, the shift would most likely be from the largely centrist or center-left *concertación* to more conservative leaders, and, if this should occur, the liberal economic policies would remain intact or even be strengthened. Elsewhere in the hemisphere, however, an extended slowdown in Chile's economy would more likely lead to anti-liberal economic pressures. The anti-globalists could then assert, "See, I told you so." Just what the new policies would be is hard to predict given the vague nature of the proposals so far, plus the reversion to economic orthodoxy by some of the most fiery advocates for change as they succeed politically—such as Lula and Lucio Gutierrez.

This analysis has implications for U.S. policy. The sidetracking of high-level attention to Latin America that followed the events of 9/11 could be costly. Continued economic stagnation in the region would not only prejudice U.S. exports and slow capital flows to the region, but would most likely lead to political changes that would not be welcome in Washington. The FTAA itself could come under pressure because it is premised on a liberal development model that might not hold sway in the future.

The logical conclusion of this analysis is that the top level of official Washington must be less rigid in its policies. Countries whose fundamental economic policies are sound, like Chile, are going through a hard period; the slowdown in the developed countries leads to magnified repercussions in the developing countries of Latin America; and U.S. goals in the hemisphere will not be achieved if the region continues to stagnate. Put in programmatic terms, the U.S. market must be more open to Latin America's goods and services, and the United States should show a less grudging disposition to help financially when crises erupt.

39 FTAA PROSPECTS*

In the title, I used the initials FTAA—an abbreviation that all trade junkies will recognize but probably seems Washington insider gobble-dygook to most Americans and, I suspect, to most Latin Americans, even when translated into the Spanish version, ALCA (Área de Libre Comercio de las Américas). The idea of the Free Trade Area of the Americas has been around since at least the Miami Summit of 1994, and much work has been done to make the FTAA a reality. My guess is that a hemispheric free trade agreement will come into existence, perhaps even by its scheduled date at the close of 2004. The reasons for this judgment are that the United States is pushing hard for the FTAA, duty-free access to the U.S. market is crucial for the majority of Latin American and Caribbean countries, and this open access to their largest market will help LAC countries attract the foreign investment they need to aug-ment their relatively low level of domestic savings. The issue is an im-portant one even if the general public is oblivious to what is going on.

There are, however, formidable obstacles to concluding the FTAA by the end of 2004. The most serious of these is probably the high level of U.S. domestic support of agriculture, a subsidy that has a profound impact on the ability of LAC countries to export competitive agricul-tural products into the United States and third markets, and even un-dercuts the ability of many Latin American producers to compete in their own countries. As this is being written, pig and poultry producers in Mexico are up in arms against the scheduled elimination of tariffs under NAFTA on imports from the United States on the grounds that U.S. producers benefit from highly subsidized feedstuffs. The Brazilians have made improved access to the U.S. market for processed agricul-tural products a condition of their acceptance of the FTAA. The United States ostensibly believes in the free market, but not really when it comes to agriculture for which substantial subsidies are the norm.

The European Union and Japan are even more culpable in support-ing their farmers. The EU also employs export subsidies to avoid accu-mulating excessive stockpiles of many agricultural commodities, a practice that adversely affects U.S. producers as well as those from LAC

---

* *Issues in International Political Economy*, no. 36 (December 2002).

countries. The Doha Round of trade negotiations taking place in Geneva under the auspices of the World Trade Organization is now going on and is scheduled to terminate at the same time as the FTAA negotiations. It has become accepted wisdom that the United States will not deal with agricultural subsidies in the FTAA discussions because the EU and Japan do not participate in these but, instead, will reserve this major negotiating issue for the WTO so that concessions can be obtained from all the major free-trade sinners. The only problem is that the French and Germans have agreed that the EU subsidies will continue until at least 2006, well after the scheduled termination date of both the Doha Round and the FTAA negotiations. No negotiations on this aspect of agriculture in Geneva and no negotiation in the FTAA because this is reserved for the WTO. This is Catch 22 writ large.

Is there any way around this obstacle? One idea is to agree in the FTAA negotiations to prohibit agricultural export subsidies in the Western Hemisphere and, in order to make this effective, to impose countervailing duties on any directly subsidized agricultural sales entering into hemispheric countries. The office of the U.S. Trade Representative is surely reluctant to agree to this because there is a "peace" pact with the EU on agriculture. But the peace essentially keeps in place an unsatisfactory situation that imperils both the FTAA and the Doha Round. In addition, the countervailing duties may have to be quite large. The Latin Americans first proposed the idea of a subsidy-free hemisphere. Another idea is to reduce U.S. import impediments on specific agricultural products coming from LAC countries. Here the problem is the existence of powerful U.S. interests unwilling to make concessions on products, such as orange juice and tobacco from Brazil and sugar from anywhere.

Is an FTAA possible without a major agricultural component, leaving agriculture to a later date in the WTO? The history of past trade negotiations in the General Agreement on Tariffs and Trade (the predecessor of the WTO) is that the United States regularly threatened to terminate negotiations if agricultural trade was not substantially liberalized, only to conclude each negotiation without much progress in liberalizing agricultural trade. The reason for this repeated capitulation was that there were many other important U.S. objectives, such as trade in nonagricultural goods, trade in services, and, more recently, intellectual property protection. This same reasoning applies to the FTAA. Brazil, in particular, has many nonagricultural products that it can—and to a large extent, *must*—export to the United States if it is to achieve its trade/development aspirations. Mexico's exports are now largely manufactured goods, as are the exports of other LAC countries.

One other problematic issue hovering between the FTAA and Doha Round relates to the use of anti-dumping (AD) measures. These are used extensively by certain U.S. industries—steel in particular—and industries in other countries. If the United States is to make major changes in its AD proceedings, it will want global and not just hemispheric quid pro quos. This is a sensitive issue in LAC countries, which are convinced that many new products exported successfully into the U.S. market are confronted with AD charges, which can impede their exports even if the case is later dismissed. The cost of defending against these charges is high for small LAC exporters. Will AD issues have to wait until 2006 or later as well because there may be no Doha Round completion before then? Most likely they will, but there may be some marginal adjustments on AD that can be made in the FTAA. AD, however, is a less of a deal-breaking issue than agriculture.

I argued earlier that I thought the FTAA would come into existence because most LAC countries wanted reasonably assured access to the U.S. market. Because of NAFTA, Mexico has this assurance and, consequently, is generally believed to be indifferent to the creation of the FTAA. It might even be considered antagonistic if one were to probe a little deeper, although unwilling to give voice to this lest it antagonize other LAC countries—then Mexico would have to share its privileged position. The United States has completed a free-trade negotiation with Chile and will soon open free-trade negotiations with Central America. The question arises whether, once these countries have achieved their objective of assured access to the United States, they will still have any great interest in concluding the FTAA. "Probably not" is the answer, at least for Central America. We may be setting up a situation for hemispheric free trade to be achieved by U.S. free-trade agreements with one or a few countries at a time, rather than all at once.

The FTAA, in my view, is as much a political as it is an economic enterprise. The basis of this assertion is that trade and investment are the only powerful instruments available to the United States for cementing its relations with the LAC region. Most of the rest of the relationship is about U.S. demands—destroying coca crops on the ground, fighting narcotics traffic, working to limit money laundering, taking action against international terrorists. The United States is no longer a large

aid donor in the Western Hemisphere, save in Colombia to limit narcotics traffic and to deal with terrorism. The United States has also
demonstrated its reluctance to mount financial rescue packages when
these are needed in the hemisphere. In an almost unique way, assurance
of an open U.S. market plays to an LAC objective, whereas no other
U.S. policy tool really does this. Trade, by elimination, has become the
tool of choice for demonstrating U.S. interest in its hemisphere.

The FTAA is a trade agreement in name but, in reality, it is probably
more an agreement that helps LAC countries attract foreign investment. The LAC countries, as noted above, are not big savers and they
need capital inflows to meet their investment and development needs.
The domestic markets are small in most LAC countries, which means
that investment generally serves to produce goods for export. Mexico,
which has a relatively large domestic market, has also transformed itself into a major exporter. Brazil, which also has a large domestic market in the Latin American context, has yet to become a significant
exporter, and this will have to take place if Brazil is to meet its development aspirations. Membership in the FTAA would thus serve Brazil
well in meeting this goal.

The U.S. government regularly stresses the importance of promoting democracy in the hemisphere, improving the region's educational
systems, lowering its poverty level, and reducing its corruption—all of
which are worthy goals. But the United States has little to offer in these
areas other than cost-free pronouncements. In trade and investment,
by contrast, the U.S. government and its private sector have to deliver
something—an open market and capital flows—and these are things
that the LAC countries cannot do for themselves. For these, they need
the United States as a partner.

40 LATIN AMERICA'S HERD BEHAVIOR*

In the 1960s and 1970s, just about every Latin American country adopted import-substituting industrialization (ISI) as the path to economic development. This was also a time of severe export pessimism across the region; the reasoning was that it was futile to promote exports to industrial countries (read the United States) because nontariff import barriers would inevitably frustrate success in this effort. Never mind that Asian countries were growing by leaps and bounds based largely on growth of exports to the United States and other industrial countries. Latin America, the argument went, was different.

This combination of high import protection and disdain for export expansion lasted for several decades only to change 180 degrees in the mid-1980s and 1990s in favor of liberal economic policies involving unilateral reduction of import impediments and a drive to promote exports as one of the keys to development. The ISI period was characterized by a disdain for foreign investment, whereas this investment was actively sought during the liberal period. We are now moving toward some third model, still inchoate, brought on by what is widely perceived as a failure of neoliberalism—the "neo" is intended to be a pejorative prefix for reasons that are not evident to me.

Even more unclear is why just about all the Latin American countries—some small, others large; some rich in natural resources, others less so; some with generally educated populations, others with high illiteracy rates—adopted these policies in unison. Brazil had a large internal market and this made ISI feasible for many industries, but Ecuador and Bolivia surely could not make ISI work in their limited internal markets. What converted a whole hemisphere from distrust of large, foreign corporations operating in their midst to active courting of these firms with tax concessions and other subsidies? It was an article of faith in the earlier period that public utilities—water, electricity, gas—should be publicly operated for the common good, only to see a wave of privatization during the more recent liberal period.

These common development policy shifts across the whole region contributed to generally synchronous economic performance. The

* Issues in International Political Economy, no. 37 (January 2003).

1980s were dreadful years in Latin America; the first half of the 1990s was relatively good; and economic growth has been awful since then. According to preliminary data from the Economic Commission for Latin America and the Caribbean, GDP per capita declined in Latin America in 2002 by 1.9 percent and is projected to improve somewhat in 2003 to a per capita decline of only 0.3 percent. It is this recent disappointing economic outcome that is leading to the call to change current policies. All the problems have not been created internally; there have been external shocks, but these acted on economies in the region that were collectively weak.

Many analysts have sought to explain Latin American behavior, although each in ways that are not fully convincing. The economic logic on which import-substituting industrialization was based was that the terms of trade deteriorated inexorably for exporters of primary exports (that is, the prices received for their exports declined in relation to the prices of industrial goods they had to import); therefore, these countries should shift to industrial production. There were, however, countries outside the region that prospered based on primary product exports. The political logic of ISI and export pessimism was the dependency theory, that the rich countries (the center, as they were called) deliberately rigged the world system to exploit the poor countries (the periphery), and this required some disconnect from the center. Here again, the Asian countries thrived by engaging with the center and penetrating their markets.

Other observers attributed the relative lack of economic success in Latin America to cultural conditioning. The countries were Catholic (a play on Max Weber's Protestant ethic) and consequently were not ethically attuned to stressing economic growth. This argument breaks down because Catholic countries in Europe did develop and so did non-Protestant countries in Asia. Another argument has been that Latin America is too religious, which is patently not the case; the religiosity of Latin American populations is not much different from that in Europe and less than in the United States.

Another approach to the cultural thesis is that Latin American countries were taken over by colonial masters from Spain and Portugal who fostered a social and governmental structure of elites versus the indigenous or mestizo masses, and this in turn led to authoritative and nondemocratic institutions designed to benefit the masters. There is much to this argument; the ex-British colonies in North America developed differently from the ex-Spanish and ex-Portuguese dependencies. However, this does not explain why the evolution into more democratic and egalitarian structures took so many centuries—and remains incomplete in Latin America even today—even as other immigrants arrived from England, Germany, Italy, and elsewhere, with different cultural traditions. When things go wrong in Latin America, there is still much longing for the rescuer on a white horse, something evident from public opinion polls and examples like Juan Perón in Argentina and Hugo Chávez in Venezuela today.

It can be argued that the herd instinct in policy constructs across the region comes from a common political and economic heritage and that each country consequently structured its society from a single template. Socially, this model led to wealthy European-origin minorities dominating impoverished indigenous and imported masses, rapacious and corrupt political leaders intent on self-empowerment and self-enrichment, a form of exploitative capitalism, one with states in cahoots with the rich and powerful and run for their benefit, and political parties that were shells designed to enrich the already rich and ignore growing poverty. Latin American countries are highly unequal in income distribution, more so than in Asia, where the economic model was different. I have deliberately stated this thesis starkly, although reality is surely much murkier.

There is one additional element in this picture that analysts point to, namely, the pressure that came from the center countries to prevent or even slow change in this structure. The United States interfered in Latin America to prevent elected leaders who were antithetical to the prevailing political-economic structure from taking office in Guatemala, the Dominican Republic, and Chile. This reinforced the tendency to uniformity of economic and political policy in Latin America by preventing those who sought change from bringing this about.

Still, historical conditioning is an important element of any country's current economic, political, and social practices, it is also necessary to take into account the changing scene. There was a significant shift to electoral democracy in Latin America in the later 1980s and 1990s. Thus, even though many of these democracies are dicey, the fragility relates to maintaining and not to obtaining democracy. Now that democracy exists in electoral terms in almost all Latin American countries, the future challenge is most likely to be in democratic deepening—in such areas as the formation of viable political parties, assuring legislative and judicial independence, reducing corruption, and holding office holders accountable.

Today, despite the disappointment with neoliberalism and the desire for some kind of change in country after country, there is clear recognition that the return to the old inward looking, export-pessimistic model is not feasible. It is difficult, therefore, to predict what economic policy changes will take place. My guess is that more attention will be paid to social issues, like education, health care, and alleviation of poverty. All of these require sustained economic growth to generate the resources for improvements in these areas, and to provide meaningful job opportunities to the poor—and this, in turn, demands policies conducive to economic growth.

It is also unclear whether the past herd tendency toward policy formulation will alter. My own guess is that it will not, at least not for a time. There is much that impels countries to adopt similar policies. Economic integration requires consultation among the member countries of these arrangements and this encourages uniformity. Disparate exchange-rate structures can lead to disaster in an integration scheme, as Brazil and Argentina learned. The similar cultural experiences of many Latin American countries pull them in the same direction when designing policy. Nevertheless, individual countries in the region are likely to experiment with new directions. Some will be disastrous, as is now the case in Venezuela. Some may be more successful, as one hopes will be the case of Brazil under Lula. The herding is unlikely to disappear, but there may be more deviations than in the past; there may be some cats that will resist being herded.

41 MEXICO: THE COST OF OUTDATED NATIONALISM*

The subject that most caught my attention on a recent visit to Mexico was the high cost that Mexico is paying for its inability to adapt aspects of its nationalism to the current situation. The particular issue that brought on this reaction was the inability of the Fox administration, and the Zedillo administration before it, to alter the ingrained conviction that oil, natural gas, and energy production must be state-owned with little private-enterprise involvement, whether domestic or foreign. Mexico now imports natural gas, whereas there is solid evidence that, with the proper investment, the country could be self-sufficient, and also bring in rather than spend foreign exchange for this product. Electricity generation is almost exclusively in the hands of state-owned enterprises and the cost is high. The future is bleak in terms of gas-powered electric energy output, and this could severely compromise the country's future growth. Pemex lacks the funds to explore and exploit the country's gas potential, even that which is not associated with oil production. I will return to this point, but Pemex's lack of capital to further develop Mexico's oil industry points to another serious structural problem.

The situation is well known, but the combination of history, tradition, and emotion results in policy stultification. The nationalism surrounding oil and gas ownership, exploration, and exploitation, and even the retail distribution of gasoline, was born in an era when the situation was radically different from what it is today. Not too many years ago, the government was unable to reclassify certain petrochemicals to permit majority foreign ownership. This was another example of oil nationalism. When the North American Free Trade Agreement was signed, Mexico for the most part chose to omit key energy issues from its provisions. Canada, by contrast, included energy, involving even a commitment to share energy with the United States at times of shortage and crisis.

Over the years, Mexico shed many of its earlier taboos. It joined the General Agreement on Tariffs and Trade in 1986 after rejecting membership a few years earlier. The president who made the earlier rejection

---

* *Issues in International Political Economy*, no. 38 (February 2003).

decision, José López Portillo, essentially opted for Mexico to be a free rider on the international trading system. Mexico entered into a free-trade agreement with the United States in 1994 after earlier categorical refusal to consider such a close economic relationship with its powerful neighbor. Mexican law and policy barely tolerated foreign direct investment for many years, but then shifted to actually seeking such investment starting in the 1980s. Mexican policy in the decades before the 1990s was to avoid any direct discussion with the United States on migration, despite the importance of this issue to millions of Mexicans; then there was a 180-degree shift in strategy under President Fox, who, as we know, made migration the foremost issue in Mexico's relations with the United States. Mexico obviously is able to change direction on key issues, but important—indeed critical—exceptions remain.

The buildup of beliefs that have such large emotional and cultural content as to make it hard to alter attitudes is hardly unique to Mexico. Senator Trent Lott demonstrated recently that he had not really shed the social outlook of his youth. Religious zealots of many persuasions are rarely amenable to changes in their cultural outlooks. My focus here, however, is on Mexico and what it must do to further its economic growth.

As I examine the Mexican scene, the danger I see is that many of its policies risk a sacrifice of its growth potential. A highly professional team in the treasury and the central bank manages Mexico's macroeconomic policy. Those who follow Latin America's financial markets give Mexico high marks for maintaining effective fiscal and monetary balance. Inflation last year exceeded its target, but only modestly—due in part to high energy prices. The peso gained strength over the past several years and has been weakening more recently, but there is no expectation that the peso will go off the deep end, as it did in 1994. The relatively clean float and a monetary policy based on inflation targeting inspire confidence in investors—internal and external. Mexico has become a formidable trading nation, perhaps overly reliant on the U.S. market, but its export products are much more varied than they were before the trade policy changes of the 1980s. Total exports of goods last year exceeded $160 billion, more than 85 percent of which were manufactures. Mexico is no longer an oil economy, but oil still plays a crucial role in running the government.

The country's major economic and social problems relate to its unsatisfactory overall economic performance. Real GDP last year grew by only 1.1 percent, which translated into a decline in per capita GDP. The GDP growth estimate for this year is higher—somewhere between 2 and 3 percent— which even at the upper figure would bring only modest per capita growth. Job growth in 2002 was insufficient to satisfy all the entrants into the labor market. The official explanation for the lack of economic growth is that, because of Mexico's high reliance on the U.S. market (which in 2002 took 83 percent of Mexico's merchandise exports), the slowdown in U.S. growth was the culprit. The unsatisfactory economic performance of the United States undoubtedly was and is a factor in Mexico's slow growth. But Mexico's structural problems contributed even more to the poor performance. Canada is even more reliant than Mexico on the U.S. market, but Canada grew by 3.5 percent in 2002.

Mexicans complain about high taxes, which are true on paper, but the fact is that tax collections amount to only 11–12 percent of GDP. This is not enough to run the government and meet vital social needs for education and health care. Pemex's contribution to government revenues amounts to 6 percent or so of GDP—more than half as much as all other taxes together. Pemex should contribute resources to the government; all oil companies pay royalties, even government-owned oil companies. Six percent of GDP, however, is high, at least twice as high as it should be. If Pemex could keep 3 percent of GDP more for itself, its ability to finance more exploration and exploitation would be markedly improved. However, better tax collection is not easy to accomplish; it has been tried repeatedly in recent decades with little success.

The unwillingness to permit private investment in oil and gas and in most electricity generation, coupled with the inability of Pemex and the government-owned electricity companies to meet these investment needs, puts the Mexican economy between those two well-known impossible positions—a rock and a hard place. Private investment in gas generation can be accomplished either by a constitutional amendment and/or by better tax collection to remove Pemex's need to fund the government. The latter requires a change in the mentality of Mexico's taxpayers. I think that a constitutional amendment is the easier and quicker path. There are two impediments to a constitutional amendment—political game playing in Congress and the cultural aversion to giving up the government monopoly on gas, oil, and electricity generation and distribution.

My sense is that if Mexico retains the structural impediments discussed here—as well as others not discussed but well known, such as the need for a more transparent justice system and a more flexible labor market—Mexico's GDP growth potential is not much more than about 3 percent a year on a sustained basis. If these rigidities were eliminated, the growth potential should be double that. These figures are orders of magnitude, but the message I took from Mexico was that the country could grow twice as fast on a sustained basis with adjustments rather than adhering to policies born a century ago and reinforced in the 1930s, but still being practiced in the radically different context of the twenty-first century.

With GDP growth at 1 percent (as it was in 2002) or even 2 percent (as it might be in 2003), there is no way that Mexico can meet its vital social needs. Poverty rates are high—in the range of 40 percent of the population—and poverty reduction requires steady GDP growth, year in and year out, particularly growth on a per capita basis. With growth at 6 percent a year, which Mexico achieved during its heyday years, social goals can be addressed. The following questions should be at the heart of Mexico's internal debate: How much growth is needed on a sustained basis to meet economic and social goals? What are the impediments to achieving this rate of growth? And how must we go about removing these impediments? I had the impression when I was last in Mexico that the internal discussion centered more on slogans and outdated nationalism than on addressing the salient, rational questions at the very heart of the problem.

42 PRESIDENT LULA'S UNCERTAIN PATH*

It is fascinating to observe the drama playing out in Brazil of a lifelong, left-leaning labor leader adopting mainstream economic measures that he had long opposed now that he is president of this important country. This reflects a sentiment common in Latin America and elsewhere, "Es otra cosa con guitarra." (Loosely translated: It's different when you must perform.) Luis Inácio "Lula" da Silva ran for president from the left three times before he was elected in his fourth try; but this time he shifted gradually to the center during his campaign and then, when he took office, endorsed measures that are important elements of the Washington Consensus, a policy prescription that is commonly derided by Latin America's intellectual left. Lula had better succeed in his presidency because if he fails, his old allies will never let him forget this policy change.

Brazil, under Lula, agreed with the IMF to raise the country's primary fiscal surplus (i.e., before taking interest payments into account) from 3.75 to 4.25 percent of GDP. This is designed to keep Brazil's debt from growing further, but also has the obvious effect of limiting the government's discretionary spending, including for social programs. "Gruel before jam" is how the *Economist* described this. The central bank has twice raised the country's reference interest rate, the Selic, since Lula assumed office. The Selic rate is now 26.5 percent, and this is high both in nominal and real terms. The main motive was to stem the growth in inflation. The inflation target for this year is 8.5 percent, but few market watchers expect it to be this low. On a recent visit to Sao Paulo, analysts from one important Brazilian bank told me that this—containing the growth of inflation—might be Lula's main challenge. Union wage bargaining becomes intense in April, and it will be hard to restrain large nominal wage increases in the face of rising inflation.

Lula's reform agenda puts social security and tax reform at the top of his agenda, particularly reform of Brazil's public-sector pension system. Lula's party, the Labor Party (PT), opposed such reform when it was proposed by President Fernando Henrique Cardoso, and the ironic argument that it stands a better chance of success now than before is precisely because it is being pushed by a PT president. This difficult

---

* *Issues in International Political Economy*, no. 39 (March 2003).

reform proposal is coming early in the Lula administration when the president's prestige is high. The government has proposed a modest Zero Hunger program, one that will not bust the budget, and it is seen as a harbinger for what may come later when the budget permits. This builds on programs instituted by Lula's predecessor, President Cardoso. Social programs like this were once seen as the bread-and-butter issues of a Lula presidency. They might still be—but not now. Unlike supply-side diehards in the United States, Lula does not believe he has the luxury of declaring that budget deficits don't matter.

President Lula (as he is called in Brazil) demonstrated that he understood he could not ignore the natural conservatism of world money-market players when he selected people for economic positions in his cabinet and in the central bank. The minister of finance, Antônio Palocci, is a member of the PT, but one reason for his appointment was that he was seen as "safe" by business and financial interests both in Brazil and elsewhere. As the *Economist* pointed out, Palocci, immediately after his appointment, traveled to the United States to urge the big banks to keep open their credit lines to Brazil. Lula's choice to head Brazil's central bank was Henrique de Campos Meirelles, president of Bank-Boston and FleetBoston's Global Bank. Lula did not slight the PT in his cabinet appointments (18 of 29 cabinet appointments came from the PT), but it is clear that special care was taken in selecting those responsible for making macroeconomic policy decisions.

Lula won the presidency because he promised change, not just in his speeches, but also because of his very background—a poor boy with little formal education who rose to prominence by his energy and wits and has long demonstrated his sympathy for the downtrodden in his work, history, and outlook. His public popularity actually increased sharply after he won the election, and it became clear that he would be given a long honeymoon to demonstrate that he would make a difference to the average Brazilian. Just how long this honeymoon will last is unknown, but surely not more than a year.

Yet, during this year, he will be hobbled by the budgetary stringency imposed by the need not to grow Brazil's debt, especially the foreign currency debt or that tied to short-term interest rates. He may not succeed fully in either his tax or pension reform proposals, and this could tarnish his image as an agent of change. The enormous inequality of incomes and opportunities in Brazil cannot be altered in a year—or four or even eight years in office. Lawlessness, crime, and drug use are all growing, and after a year or so in office, this growth will likely be attributed to Lula's inability to deliver desired economic and social benefits.

Tensions are deep in the society. They exist between the political parties, between the established elites and the new economic and social managers appointed by Lula, and between the hard liners in the PT and the pragmatists who are advocating mainstream economic policies for now. Almost 30 percent of the PT deputies in the Congress are from the far left. Yet, a great majority of the population wants Lula to succeed, as was clear in the election and subsequent opinion polls. Many financial and business people with whom I spoke when in Sao Paulo volunteered the sentiment that Brazil, if it is to have a prosperous future, must relieve the deep poverty and reduce the vast income inequality that exists. Lip service? Perhaps. But also, I think, a sign that they want Lula to succeed because if he doesn't, who knows what comes next.

This is the central theme of a survey of Brazil in the *Economist* of February 23, 2003, that carried the title "Make or break." Or as the author of the survey put it, it is possible to foresee two drastic outcomes: a "dream" scenario in which Lula succeeds in carrying out basic societal reforms; or a "nightmare" scenario in which the future is growing crime and rising poverty. A crucial requirement of the dream scenario is a growing GDP, one that provides more resources for the budget, helps create jobs, and reduces poverty. If one tries to understand why the left-leaning labor leader chose to start his administration with mainstream economic measures, this is the answer: Brazil cannot prosper, cannot get outside support, cannot attract investment, unless the government is seen as being responsible in handling economic fundamentals. Few observers expect GDP growth to exceed 1 to 2 percent this year, but current policies are designed to establish a foundation for more robust growth in the years ahead. Lula's task is not easy. He must retain his credentials as an agent of social change even as his economic measures put off that change until at least next year, and he must mollify widely disparate groups in society, those who have benefited from the system and those who have had to survive from the dregs that remained.

The U.S. government has played this transformation quite professionally, something one might not have anticipated given the indifference toward Brazil that prevailed earlier. Much of the earlier relationship consisted of slugging it out on specific trade issues—Brazil's policy on restricting U.S. investment and imports in the computer industry, for example, and U.S. agricultural subsidies and import restrictions on key Brazilian products. Those of us in Washington who follow U.S. policy toward Brazil used to joke that official visitors from each country came with a list of trade complaints and that that mindset framed the bilateral interaction. Knowledge of Brazil in the U.S. Congress was scant and few congressional visits to Brazil took place. There were even some offensive anti-Lula congressional pronouncements during the campaign. This surface knowledge was surprising because the U.S. business community had long since discovered Brazil, which was the largest destination for U.S. direct investment in Latin America. It was hard to fathom this official inattention to a country of 175 million people with an extensive industrial complex.

When Lula was elected, the administration welcomed his ascension to the presidency, and Lula visited with President Bush in Washington. The emissary that the Bush administration sent to Lula's inauguration was a cabinet-level official, Robert Zoellick, the United States Trade Representative; this was not bad, but not optimal because it tended to frame the relationship largely in trade terms at a time when much more is at stake. Many Latin American countries are going through difficult times in retaining their democratic institutions, and here was the largest of all the regional countries peacefully and democratically choosing a new president. Trade is important, but the U.S.-Brazilian relationship should extend more deeply into political, social, and global issues befitting the two largest countries in the Western Hemisphere.

Just a word on trade issues. Brazil—including Lula—has been ambiguous about its support of the Free Trade Area of the Americas (FTAA). Nevertheless, the reality is that Brazil is participating in the deliberations and jointly chairs the overall negotiation process with the United States. Brazil's final decisions about the FTAA are uncertain, but then so are those of the United States.

43 STRAINS IN THE CANADA-U.S. RELATIONSHIP*

It has been hard in recent months to keep up with Canadian commentary on relations with the United States because there has been so much of it. Much of the discussion revolves around the optimum techniques to deal with the joint terrorist threat while doing minimal damage to the movement of goods, services, and people—and this commentary is unexceptionable, indeed constructive. Other writings deal with Canadian concerns that their views are given short shrift by leading U.S. policymakers and consist of suggestions on how to overcome this neglect. Again, this is useful, as ideas are publicly debated. Finally, much writing is a mixture of explanations and attacks on the Canadian government's decision not to support the U.S. position on Iraq, and many of these declarations raise fears of possible U.S. retaliatory actions, especially in economic relations. This sort of bilateral tension is not new—it existed during the years 1968–1979 and 1980–1984 when Pierre Trudeau was prime minister. It is troublesome, nonetheless, because there are hardly any other two countries—and maybe none—that have been such fortunate neighbors.

The Canadian concern that security trumps trade arose after September 11, 2001, when Canadian trucks bearing goods experienced delays crossing the border. More than 45,000 trucks cross the border each day, and much of what they carry is destined for use almost immediately in U.S. manufacturing facilities. The just-in-time industrial production is quite advanced, especially in the automotive industry on opposite sides of the bridge between Windsor, Ontario, and Detroit, Michigan, and delays and unpredictability can be highly disruptive. Much of this trade is intra-firm or between related companies and, if the movement of production inputs from Canada is not reliable, there is no reason why the Canadian facilities cannot be moved a few miles south into the United States.

Handling the security-trade mix at the border is a highly cooperative venture, based on the "smart border" accord of December 2001, being implemented under the direction of Deputy Prime Minister John Manley and Secretary of Homeland Security Tom Ridge. For the moment, the twin imperatives of security and trade are working efficiently.

---

* *Issues in International Political Economy*, no. 40 (April 2003).

The techniques put in place would be jeopardized, however, if there were a successful terrorist incident that circumvented the border safeguards or involved terrorists moving across the border. This is why the Canadian Council of Chief Executives (CCCE) recommended reinventing the notion of border, that is, setting up a common security perimeter for the two countries. Governor George Pataki of New York and Premier Ernie Eves of Toronto made the same suggestion.

The notion of perimeter screening to speed up the movement of goods and residents of the two countries is logical on the surface, but there are inherent problems that must be considered. Without any border screening, the two countries would need identical immigration laws to permit the free movement of people from one country to the other and a common tariff and other trade restrictions so that the trans-shipment of goods from one country to the other would not matter. These steps smack of sharing sovereignty rather than "mutual respect for sovereignty," which is an essential element of the CCCE proposal. Sharing sovereignty is not necessarily a bad idea, but that is not what the CCCE advocates. A common security perimeter for Canada and the United States would omit Mexico, unless there was a common North American perimeter—something that would multiply ancillary complications many times over.

U.S. policymakers might not neglect Canada, some Canadians have suggested, if some "big ideas" were adopted, as phrased by Allan Gotlieb, a well-known personality in Canada and a former ambassador to the United States. The big idea of transforming the free trade area that exists between Canada and the United States into a customs union (i.e., having a common external tariff) was suggested in a study written by Wendy Dobson for Canada's C. D. Howe Institute. Having a common perimeter would be a much bigger idea because, in my judgment, this would necessarily require both a common tariff and free movement of people. A Canada-U.S. customs union would complicate North American unity under NAFTA because the U.S.-Mexican relationship would continue to be one of free trade without a common tariff. Mexico would be reluctant to enter into a North American customs union because this would require terminating its free trade agreement with the European Union.

There is probably much truth to Canada's perception that its views are largely neglected in the United States. In other words, the relationship is seen largely in the United States as one of trade and investment and not much more. The big idea stimulated by this situation is that Canada build up its defense posture for the common defense of North America. Canada has done just the opposite in recent years; it has built down its military and devoted the resources to social issues and budgetary balance instead. The CCCE has stated that Canada must make a vastly more effective contribution to the defense and security of the North American homeland. Jack Granatstein, a Canadian historian, has said that "whether Canadians realize it or not, Canada is now all but undefended." The choice to focus on social and economic issues may be a reasonable one, but it does have its consequences. Canada, in this sense, is now much like Mexico—an important neighbor with which there is much trade but which does not contribute much to the common defense. Under these circumstances, it is not surprising that Canada's voice on national security issues does not have much resonance. It is mere opinion with few resources to back it up.

The bilateral relationship was severely strained by Canada's decision not to support the U.S. position in Iraq. Canada, of course, was not unique, but as two Canadian scholars (Bill Dymond and Michael Hart) have written, Canada by its action removed its name from the list of countries that can be counted as reliable partners and principled U.S. allies. Canadian authorities make a number of points to soften the perception that Canada does not contribute to the common defense. They point out that Canadian frigates and aircraft patrol the Persian Gulf to assure maritime passage; that Canada will be sending 2,000 new troops to help in security stability in Afghanistan; and, in March, Canada announced a $100 million humanitarian aid package for the Iraqi people.

In late March, U.S. ambassador to Canada Paul Celluci stated in a speech that the United States was disappointed that Canada was not doing enough in the war. A week later, he adopted a softer tone and stated that the economic ties between the two countries are too deep to be interrupted for any period of time. The implication of the first speech was that there might be trade punishment against Canada by the United States; the second speech implied that this would not take place. Cellucci also suggested that he made his first speech under instructions from Washington. In my view, this was a most unwise speech.

Trade issues are central to the Canada-U.S. relationship. About 85 percent of Canada's exports go to the United States, and they constitute more than 35 percent of Canada's GDP. About 70 percent of the trade is either intra-firm or between related parties in the two countries so that any restrictions would immediately affect U.S. as well as Canadian companies. The amount of merchandise that now moves between the two countries is more than U.S.$1.2 billion a day. It is hard to exaggerate the implications of imposing trade restrictions for the two countries, and it is not an overstatement to assert that even an implied threat by the United States to take such steps is madness. I assume therefore that it will not happen, except for marginal actions by small producers and traders.

Canadian columnist Jeffrey Simpson has written that the tension that exists in Canada about its interests and instincts with respect to the United States is greater than at any time since World War II. As Simpson put it, Canada's instincts are those of continental Europe, and its interests are aligned with those of the United States. Foreign policy, he argued, is about instincts, and economics is about interests. Although these tensions have long existed in Canada, they are now being pushed to their limit. It is time, therefore, for both nations to cool their rhetoric, which is what Ambassador Cellucci's second speech was intended to do. The relationship is too important and too valuable for both countries to let it slip into lasting resentments.

44 U.S.–LATIN AMERICAN ATTITUDES: MISTRUST AND INDIFFERENCE*

The United States found few supporters among Latin American countries for its position during the run-up to the war in Iraq. The main annoyance in the U.S. government centered on Mexico and Chile because they were members of the United Nations Security Council when the U.S.-UK-Spain second resolution on the use of force against Iraq came up, and these countries indicated they would have voted "no" had the resolution not been withdrawn. Official U.S. displeasure has since manifested itself in a variety of ways: the lack of any direct communication between President Bush and President Fox of Mexico; and the delay in signing the completed free trade agreement with Chile even as the United States went ahead with the Singapore FTA.

Other than the anticipated compulsion to cast votes in the Security Council, there was little difference between the attitudes of Mexico and Chile as compared with the rest of Latin America. Opinion polls taken at that time in other key countries showed that public sentiment was against the U.S. position. In Brazil, the anti-U.S. majority was more than 80 percent; in Argentina it was 85 percent. The comparable anti-U.S. sentiment was 90 percent in Mexico and 85 percent in Chile. The major exception to this attitude was Colombia, which enjoys U.S. support in fighting its own internal guerrilla movements. Public sentiment on this issue in Latin America was not much different from that in other regions, such as Europe, Asia, and the Middle East.

There is a long history of tension in U.S.-Latin American relations, however, that goes back more than a century and a half, and one has to ask why this has been so. U.S. independence as a nation came slightly earlier than it did generally in Latin America. The governing elites in both areas were European—British essentially in the United States and Canada, and Spanish and Portuguese in Latin America—but political and economic developments in the two regions have diverged from the outset. I will not get into all the reasons that might explain this divergence, except to note that one outcome of this has been tense public attitudes between the two regions.

---

* *Issues in International Political Economy*, no. 41 (May 2003).

Was this inevitable, given their different post-independence experiences? Probably yes. But these differences were aggravated by 150 years of actions that made common sentiments near impossible.

The accepted cliché is that Latin Americans have love-hate feelings toward the United States. Latin Americans, as this analysis goes, love U.S. openness and creature comforts but hate U.S. arrogance. The words "love" and "hate" are too stark, however; respect for U.S. democracy and openness coexist with resentment of U.S. actions. There is considerable annoyance with U. S. pretensions of superiority.

We in the United States have long understood the existence of these attitudes and from time to time have sought to dispel or soften them, as in the Good Neighbor policy of the 1930s and the Alliance for Progress of the 1960s. U.S. attitudes toward Latin America are so ingrained, however, that our policies to moderate them do not last long. At their core is the U.S. perception that Latin American nations are not U.S. equals, have not developed successful economies, and are only now—after more than 150 years—shedding authoritarian and military rule. Deep down, I believe that Americans are unlikely to treat Latin American nations with the dignity and equality they seek until those nations demonstrate that they can achieve consistent economic growth under entrenched democratic systems.

Demonstrations of the condescending behavior of the U.S. government can be cited endlessly. There are sporadic U.S. efforts to demonstrate that we know Latin America is down there, south of us, and that the countries and people have their own developmental and political aspirations. But U.S. attention to the region is like a person on one side of a seesaw—it all depends on circumstance whether he is up or down. The Alliance for Progress was a reaction to Castro's takeover of the Cuban government. U.S. attention on Central America exploded during the Cold War when we feared the influence of the Soviet Union, and largely disappeared after that. President Jimmy Carter promoted human rights in Latin America and, although the region's authoritarian leaders resented these intrusions, much of the citizenry welcomed them. The U.S. government has all but ignored Latin America since 9/11. It had no inhibitions in invading countries to bring about regime change: the Dominican Republic, Grenada, and Panama are relatively recent examples. None of those regimes was estimable, but we felt freer to intervene in Latin America than against equally obnoxious regimes in other parts of the world.

Congressional actions on Latin America are sometimes just plain unthinking. Within the past few days, Representative Cass Ballenger (R-N.C.) offered an amendment to a non-binding resolution that stated that any agreement on migration between Mexico and the United States should also include an accord to open Petróleos Mexicanos to investment by U.S. oil companies and reforms to make Pemex's operations more transparent and efficient. In light of the emotional feelings in Mexico about public ownership of oil resources, this kind of gratuitous command can only serve to complicate President Fox's political task of convincing his opposition to reform Mexico's natural gas and electricity generation structure. How would the U.S. Congress react if a Mexican legislator linked Mexico's willingness to open its market to corn-fructose imports from the United States to action on immigration matters? Or to improvements in the U.S. health care system, which is undoubtedly more incoherent and costly than are Pemex's operations?

By now, we are all familiar with the findings of the Pew Research Center's study on global attitudes toward the United States. These public opinion surveys found that although a large reservoir of goodwill toward the United States remains in most countries, favorability ratings have fallen since 2000 in 19 of the 27 countries where benchmarks are available. In Latin America, where majorities in most countries retain a positive view of the United States, favorable opinion has declined since 2000 in 7 of the 8 countries surveyed. This ambiguity in sentiment toward the United States not only has a long history, but the findings are highly sensitive to recent circumstances—such as the U.S. position in Iraq.

Two pragmatic questions remain: (1) Do these ambiguous attitudes in Latin America toward the United States matter? (2) If they do, what can be done about the problem?

Part of the answer to the first question is that the U.S. government sometimes thinks that these attitudes matter very much. The Alliance for Progress demonstrated this. So did the Reagan administration's efforts to prevent entrenchment of governments that supported the Soviet Union during the Cold War. The positions of Chile and Mexico in the Security Council were based on public opposition in those countries to the U.S. resolution, and President Vicente Fox of Mexico had the added problem of an upcoming congressional election—but, nevertheless, the United States was annoyed by the lack of support for its Iraq position. Had public attitudes in the two countries been different, had their publics supported the U.S. stance, their positions in the Security Council surely would have been more favorable to the United States.

The main reason we must care about public attitudes in Latin America toward the United States is that we share a hemisphere. We have been the hegemon on this continent and would prefer to lead by example and not by pressure. The U.S. government wanted the Chile FTA, and it can only be considered a foreign policy failure to allow disgruntlement over Chile's position on an extraneous issue to trump the trade position. Is a trade agreement something that we confer politically on countries, or is it intended, in and of itself, to be of mutual benefit?

As for the second question—on what we can do and what Latin America can do to moderate the swings in public sentiment toward each other—the answer is much harder to give. We cannot order the U.S. government to have a longer attention span on Latin America. Latin America has made much economic and social progress, but the process of transforming the countries from developing to developed, with sophisticated democratic structures, will not be instantaneous. We can do more to educate the U.S. public about the cultures in Latin America, especially now that we are increasing the Latino element in our own society. Equally important, we can ask U.S. legislators to please think before they speak. We can try to treat people from the region with the dignity they deserve. The U.S. president, whether Clinton or Bush, can set an example by demonstrating in speeches and through deeds that his attention to the region is consistent and durable. We can move ahead with the Free Trade Area of the Americas, which most of the countries of the region want; this is the most positive feature of our current hemispheric policy.

We can, in theory, do all of these things. We have never done so consistently in the past. But maybe we can do better, just as we want Latin American governments to do better in providing decent lives for their populations.

45 KIRCHNER AND ARGENTINA[*]

Argentina has just elected a president whose views are largely unknown. Néstor Kirchner was the governor of Santa Cruz, a small province in Patagonia, when he was handpicked as a candidate by the outgoing president, Eduardo Duhalde. This was different from the Mexican *dedazos* in that the politicians pointed to there by the outgoing president as the all-but-certain next president were invariably prominent personalities. What we know about Kirchner's thinking comes from his campaign statements, his Web site, his inaugural address, and what has been gleaned by examining his record as governor. He was not helped by the circumstance of his election by default, when his main opponent, former president Carlos Menem, withdrew just before the runoff date when his overwhelming defeat was apparent. It is not fair to say that Kirchner had the positive support of only 22 percent of the electorate (his share in the first round), but that is the way it was played by much of the Argentine media. It would have been better for all concerned if Menem had withdrawn immediately after the first round on April 27 and if Ricardo López Murphy, who came in third, had then entered the two-person runoff with Kirchner. That would have been a real election.

Kirchner inherits a horrible situation, and any reasonable person must wish him well for the sake of the Argentine people. The Argentine GDP declined by almost 11 percent last year, following a spate of declines during the previous four years. The economy now appears to be growing at a 4 percent rate for 2003, but this is based largely on exploiting unused capacity for import substitution. Using idle capacity has a short life, and significant new investment is needed for the stimulus to be more than a temporary blip. In other words, Kirchner has only a short time to instill confidence in both domestic and foreign investors—and they are notorious "show-me" types. Argentina is not paying its external debt, another situation that cannot continue much longer. Unemployment is at 21 percent, and an estimated 50 percent of the population in this once middle-class country now lives in poverty. Crime is now rampant in Buenos Aires, long reputed to be one of the safe cities in Latin America.

[*] *Issues in International Political Economy*, no. 42 (June 2003).

Kirchner's recent statements, including his inaugural address, seem to be directed at two audiences: the domestic population, to which he speaks like a populist; and the foreign community, to which he emphasizes conservative orthodoxy. This may be a political necessity—after all, there are two audiences, and no politician can long endure without catering to the one that elected him—but it makes for uncertainty as to which pronouncements will dominate when concrete actions must be taken. In his inaugural address, he advocated a large public works and housing program, in part to stimulate the economy and provide jobs quickly. On this, he cited what the United States did during the Great Depression of the 1930s. In another part of this speech he stated that the government should not spend more than it collects in revenue, that it must run fiscal activities without resort to further debt or printing more money. Which will it be, significant infrastructure spending or a balanced budget? Like the FDR administration during the depression, my guess is that the fiscal balance will go—at least for a time. As he put it in his speech, the country cannot continue to cover the deficit by "permanent" indebtedness or resort to monetary emission "without control."

Argentina, he said, is not the kind of country to base its national project on debt default, but the applause line that followed was that paying the debt could not be done at the cost of postponing access to dignified housing, secure jobs, education for the nation's children, and providing health care. He also laid down three conditions for debt restructuring: reduction of the total amount (now about $134 billion, of which about $50 billion needs rescheduling); lowering the interest rates; and lengthening the maturities. All this leaves uncertainty about how long debt restructuring and payment will be delayed. The longer it takes to do that, the more difficult it will be to secure foreign investment; and this plays back to the need to attract new investment to sustain the modest economic recovery now under way.

Brazil is Argentina's largest export market, and the combination of Brazil's devaluation in 1999 and Brazil's lackluster economic performance hit Argentina hard. Exports to Brazil and other Mercosur countries are only now showing some recovery. What Argentina should have learned is that Brazil alone is a weak reed on which to base trade policy. Argentina has not been a major trading nation. Its export-to-GDP ratio oscillated between 8 and 10 percent during the 1990s. There was a big jump in 2002 to an estimated 33 percent, but this was due not to increased exports but to the sharp decline in GDP. Argentina's trade balance improved in 2002; this again was not due to increased exports, but rather to a sharp drop in imports from $27 billion the year before to less than $14 billion. If the Argentine economy recovers, import demand will surely grow. I suspect that the hope of preventing this from happening is at the core of the stated policy of more import substitution. This may be more dream than reality.

My reading is that Argentina needs the Free Trade Area of the Americas in order to diversify its export markets. Chile and Mexico realized that it is better to have trade access to a large market than to a modest one, to have a trade agreement with a rich country and not just with relatively poor countries.

Kirchner's position on trade issues also seems to be directed to two audiences. He undoubtedly realizes that his pronouncements to an Argentine audience are available outside the country, but this is another manifestation of the dominance of domestic politics. President Kirchner's Web site contains the following statement on trade and production: "The years of uncontrolled neoliberalism without protection of work in Argentina, and of indiscriminate opening [to imports], led to the collapse of national industry and its inevitable outcome: unemployment and misery for millions of Argentines." (My translation.) This does not sound like a president prepared to enter into serious trade negotiations. On the other hand, in his inaugural address, he said that "our country must be open to the world" in what he called a "realistic manner." It will take a little time before his true intentions can be discerned.

The mostly unstated but generally understood position when Carlos Menem was president was that Argentina wanted the FTAA to succeed because that way access to the U.S. market could be assured without having to break Mercosur unity. Good political relations with Brazil are important to Argentina, and the Mercosur customs union, imperfect though it may be, provides trade benefits. Brazil's position on the FTAA has long been ambiguous and remains so under President Lula. Lula has made light of the agreed date—the end of 2005—to terminate the negotiations. Now the president of Argentina, like Lula, has stressed the primacy of Mercosur over other trade negotiations. As Kirchner put it in his inaugural address: Argentina is ready to compete in the policy of regional trade preferences, through Mercosur.

It is worth repeating Kirchner's formidable tasks. He must deal with corruption, as he said in his campaign and his inaugural address; he must end the impunity of those engaging in corrupt or other extra-legal activities; he must deal with the rising crime in big cities, especially Buenos Aires; he needs resources to improve health and educational facilities; and he must deal with the poverty that has marked Argentina since the economic collapse last year.

None of the important social goals can be achieved without a restoration of economic growth, something that has eluded the country over the past five years. What Argentina needs, however, is not just one or two years of growth. This may be attainable by delaying debt repayment, priming the fiscal pump though public works, and relying on installed industrial capacity until that gives out. Alan García did that when he became president of Peru in 1985, but after a few years the Peruvian economy hit bottom.

By the same token, Kirchner cannot practice austerity—in order to satisfy the foreign gurus who urge him to pay attention to economic fundamentals like a balanced budget and an open market—with any assurance that this will lead to more growth in two or three years. If that were Kirchner's policy, he might not be there when the promised economic growth comes. This is not an uncommon dilemma of leaders after a severe collapse. Lula faces a similar task, in that he must eventually respond to the social needs of the people who brought him to the presidency. Kirchner's task is harder; I'm not sure the word "eventually" can work for him.

Kirchner and Argentina have to work out the balance. How much public works, how much education and health care expenditures, how much deficit, how much trade protection, how much debt repayment delay—these are the critical decisions. And this complex task has been given to a political neophyte at the national level. I wish him well.

46 THE COST OF DIVISIONS WITHIN LATIN AMERICA*

There is persistent bemoaning of the lack of attention the United States pays to Latin America. The unhappiness is justified, although neglect is interspersed from time to time with excessive attention to particular countries. The failure by the United States Senate for five years to confirm an assistant secretary of state for the Western Hemisphere, rectified only a few weeks ago when Roger Noriega was confirmed, is a recent demonstration of this indifference. Latin America seemed to fall off the map in official Washington after 9/11, which was a more significant sign of neglect.

However, the lack of cohesion among Latin American and Caribbean (LAC) countries is an equally important impediment to close relations with the United States and the outside world generally. This is true within subregions of LAC as well as for the region as a whole. The Andean countries, despite the existence of an economic integration agreement among them, are constantly at one another's throats. Peru and Ecuador went to war with each other a few years ago. Venezuela under President Chávez gives every sign of supporting the guerilla groups in Colombia. One of the benefits of the U.S. free trade negotiations with the five countries of the Central American Common Market is the incentive it gives the five to reach some common policies—and, even in this context, this is proving to be difficult. The Caribbean Community every few years vows that it will become more cohesive—and just recently it vowed again to do this—and maybe one day it will. The new presidents of Brazil and Argentina promise to work together to make Mercosur the meaningful integration arrangement it has the potential to be—and perhaps they will in ways that did not prevail earlier. There is a uniform chorus from scholars in Brazil and Argentina that greater coordination of policy is needed in Mercosur, and this reflects the recognition that there was precious little coordination (or even consultation) earlier.

Do these divisions matter in terms of relations with the United States? One place they matter is in the negotiation of the Free Trade Area of the Americas. These divisions, I suspect, were not fully understood when

---

* *Issues in International Political Economy*, no. 44 (August 2003).

the proposal for hemispheric free trade was first made. Brazil sees little advantage, either politically or in trade terms, from the FTAA, whereas Central America sees more assured access to the U.S. market as vital. These differences in national positions are normal in trade negotiations. At the same time, however, they mean that the United States is not negotiating with a cohesive region, or even unified subregions, but almost country by country. The inability to join forces surely reduces the leverage of the LAC negotiators. The U.S. negotiators surely take advantage of these divisions even though they are frustrated by them at the same time.

The U.S. proposal for free trade in the Americas was an exception to the general practice of neglect of the hemisphere, but more and more one gets the impression that the initiative was instinctive rather than well thought out. The FTAA presupposes that the label "Latin America" represents an intellectual and political reality rather than a geographic configuration. This is coming out now as the countries approach the real negotiating agenda as it affects each of them. One element after another of the agenda is coming under pressure: The United States is unprepared to negotiate farm subsidies in the hemisphere; the Brazilians and others wish to exclude intellectual property; few Latin American countries are prepared to open up the full range of services (such as telecommunications) to competitive imports; differences are emerging on investment and public procurement matters. What seems to be happening is that the exclusions are likely to multiply, thereby negating the advantage of a hemisphere-wide negotiation.

The LAC countries, now that they seek to promote exports as an important engine of development, have signed bilateral and plurilateral economic integration agreements with frenzy. I have not counted how many actually exist, but there surely are at least 20, more likely 30 or more. In fact, it is hard to count the number because the agreements often take complex forms, like Bolivian association with Mercosur. The "spaghetti" description grows out of this proliferation of agreements as one draws lines on a map connecting the countries among which they exist.

Each agreement is an effort by the signatories to obtain preferential treatment in their bilateral or plurilateral trade. Each agreement, viewed this way, is a form of beggar-thy-neighbor policy and, as in the 1930s, many can and do play at this game. This multiplicity of preferential agreements is a stark example of the lack of cohesion in Latin

America. The greatest virtue the FTAA could have is to eliminate many of these agreements—each with its own rules—by subsuming them into the larger, hemisphere-wide agreement. This is unlikely to happen, however, because the FTAA is unlikely to deal comprehensively with all the trade issues involved in the bilateral agreements. It is not fair to criticize Latin America alone for the practice of preferential trade bilateralism now being emulated by the United States and long practiced by the European Union.

The lack of unity in Latin America is not new. Simon Bolívar failed at this effort. President Chávez renamed his country the Bolivarian Republic of Venezuela to publicize his desire to be an agent of Latin American unification. The issue, seen from the Bolivarian vantage, is more political than it is economic. I focus on this issue because the trade negotiations seemingly provided a way to achieve some unity, whereas the straight political approach has long proved futile. The unity of the European Union came, as is well known, from the economic approach; and I had conjectured, perhaps naively, that the trade path was the most feasible technique for Latin America to find greater unity. This route gave the LAC countries the possibility of dealing collectively with the United States. The Brazilians had come to much the same conclusion—that trade might be the lever for South American cohesion—when they embarked on seeking associates for Mercosur to gain leverage in negotiating with the United States. The Brazilians have also failed in this effort, at least thus far.

I do not want to leave the impression that the FTAA will come to naught—although it might—but rather that it is likely to be less comprehensive than originally contemplated. Even if all the issues cited above fall by the wayside, the FTAA could still end up as a market access agreement. It is hard to see the outlines of such an agreement because it will have to involve U.S. concessions on nontariff barriers in exchange for LAC concessions on tariffs, and it is far from clear that either side is prepared to go very far in these efforts. Many Latin American countries are concerned with increased imports not just from the United States but also from Brazil, and this must play itself out in the negotiations. Tariffs imposed by Brazil, to pick the most important country, are relatively high and a transition to zero in an FTAA would be beneficial for Brazil, in my judgment, as well as for the other countries of the Americas who seek to export to Brazil. If Brazil's tariffs came down, so probably would the external tariffs of Mercosur. This, if followed up by other measures to strengthen Mercosur—as Presidents Kirchner of Argentina and Lula of Brazil say they wish to do—could provide the germ for greater unity of purpose in the Southern Cone. The foregoing sentences are filled with "ifs." If the United States is prepared to give significant concessions, if Brazil is willing to open its market more widely, if Lula and Kirchner are prepared to coordinate their macroeconomic policies, if other LAC countries are prepared to reduce their import barriers—and all of this without the tradeoffs from other sectors—only then is a substantial market access agreement possible.

I have been asking myself why the trade route to greater LAC unity of purpose is not getting much traction. There are the obvious reasons: nationalistic desires to protect domestic interests; distrust among the countries, as exemplified by the disunity discussed earlier; political competition among them, say, as between Mexico and Brazil; and the disparities among the LAC countries in size, trade prowess, and feasible hemispheric ambitions. Other reasons do not immediately jump to the surface: Brazil is not sure it wants to share its hegemonic status in South America with the United States—the biggest hegemon of them all—should there be a comprehensive FTAA; there is considerable anti-Americanism in Latin America at the moment and this may be impeding the ardor for free trade in some LAC countries.

Yet, having said all this, one would think that LAC countries would do whatever they could to assure improved access to the U.S. market. This was Chile's position, and it led to Chile's free trade agreement with the United States. It is the position of Central America, the Dominican Republic, Colombia, Peru, and others. Cooperative proposals in trade matters would not compromise the sovereignties of the LAC countries. While such cooperation could lead to greater political cooperation, this is not a necessary or foreordained outcome. In any event, the situation seems to be more "each country for itself" rather than unity of purpose in the achievement of what could be a most important agreement for most LAC countries

47 PERU'S PERENNIAL PROBLEMS POP UP AGAIN[*]

Peru was in the worldwide news late last month when its Truth and Reconciliation Commission issued a report on the human cost of the terrorism and authoritarian governments over the 1980 to 2000 period. The commission was created in June 2001, and it took two years to gather the information to prepare the report. A truth and reconciliation commission is not unique to Peru; just to stay in South America, Chile had one to report on the brutality and killings of the Pinochet years,[1] and Argentina had one to deal with the years of military government and disappearances. The headline stimulated by the Peruvian commission was that more than 69,000 persons died or disappeared over the 20-year period covered, more than double the number used earlier. These were the dreadful "glory" years of Shining Path (*Sendero Luminoso*), the Tupac Amaru Revolutionary Movement, and the military response.

This report was both praised for its thoroughness and criticized by those who felt that it was too evenhanded in its criticism of Shining Path, which inflicted more suffering than any other group, and of the military and the peasant militias it trained for draconian actions to wipe out guerrilla activities. Like other such commissions, the revelations open but do not resolve the complex question of how much justice and retribution to seek against individual perpetrators as opposed to focusing on the future in order to get on with economic and political life.

The commission's report highlights how difficult and turbulent Peru's modern history has been. Peru is highly divided between the small sophisticated elite in the main cities, primarily Lima and its outskirts, and the indigenous population of its highland and jungle areas. This division, and the complex terrain, is what gave Shining Path the ability to mount the bloody campaign that it did. Many years ago, when I was visiting Cuzco, it dawned on me during a conversation with a young shoeshine boy that he knew he lived in a place called Cuzco, but he did not know that he lived in a country called Peru. This surely has changed, but not the social and economic divisions that existed then. Peru is a relatively populous country of some 27 million, of whom

[*] *Issues in International Political Economy*, no. 45 (September 2003).

about 50 percent live below the poverty line. About one-third of the population is aged 15 or less. GDP per capita is about $2,000 at market exchange rates.

Peru has experienced both authoritarian and elected leadership, but the leadership group is quite small. This is evident from the fact that the same persons appear as presidents or presidential aspirants. Fernando Belaunde Terry was president from 1963 to 1968, and again from 1980 to 1985. Alan García was president from 1985 to 1990 and did appalling damage to the economy, but he is now one of the leading contenders to succeed the current president, Alejandro Toledo Manrique, when his term expires in 2006, or before then if Toledo is unable to complete his full term. In addition, candidates seem to emerge from nowhere, as Alberto Fujimori did when he was first elected president in 1990, and even Toledo, when he was elected in 2001.

The mood of the electorate is highly changeable and, viewed from afar, quite forgiving of past actions of leaders—or perhaps the proper word is resigned to their past failures or hubris. Fujimori was reelected twice, under highly dubious circumstances in his second reelection, but then was forced out of office in 2000 because of electoral and other machinations. Toledo was elected only two years ago but, based on public opinion polls, his current popularity is only about 12 percent. The other two living perennials, Fujimori (now resident in Japan) and García (long resident in Colombia and France before returning to Peru in 2000), rank higher than Toledo in current opinion polls. Fujimori's popularity has much to do with the public perception of him as a strong leader who got things done: combating and destroying the power of Shining Path; and, as president, pulling off an *autogolpe* (a self coup) to seize authoritarian control of the government. García's popularity has much to do with his being seen as caring for the downtrodden in Peru.

There is a seeming disconnect between the high GDP growth rates in Peru under Toledo and the low esteem in which he is held by the general public. This may have something to do with his personality, or even the fact that as a person of indigenous origin he comes from a different social background than the business and power elites in Lima. But then so does Fujimori, although his Japanese origin may have been an asset— and each was a relative unknown when first elected to the presidency. Peru's GDP grew by 5.3 percent in 2002, the highest growth rate in all of Latin America for the year. Its projected GDP growth this year is still a respectable 3.5-4.0 percent, at least a percentage point higher than the rest of region.

This disparity between high overall economic growth and low public esteem most likely reflects another phenomenon—that high overall growth does not trickle down to the majority of the economy. Job creation remains low, and the informal economy remains large. Yet, if Peru is ever to meaningfully reduce its level of poverty, one essential ingredient is high overall growth, year in and year out. This, in time, will almost certainly reduce the poverty level. That, of course, does not help a sitting president with a limited term.

One of the most influential socioeconomic books in Latin America in the past 25 years was Hernando de Soto's *El Otro Sendero (The Other Path* in English). The central argument of the book was that much of the poverty in Peru was due to the failure of the authorities to give legal property rights to those operating quite openly in the informal economy—living on land and in houses to which they have no titles, operating bus lines, producing goods, selling merchandise on the streets—as a basis for them to have access to credit. Although the book had a resounding impact outside of Peru, most of the actions recommended were not implemented. De Soto also demonstrated how long it took to get things done when dealing with the government, plus the fact that bribery was also needed to get action. Based on De Soto's work, which in essence documents the daily experience of the people, it is not hard to understand why Peruvians generally have so little confidence in their institutions. This lack of confidence permeates all levels of society and is directed at all levels of public institutions.

Peru is also organizing its economy to enable the country to participate in the Free Trade Area of the Americas or, if that is long delayed, to enter into a free-trade area with the United States. Peru already enjoys trade preferences in the U.S. market under the Andean Trade Preference Act (ATPA), but an FTA would go much further in opening the U.S. market and would also involve the gradual elimination of its tariffs for most imports from the United States. In addition, an FTA is a form of contract, whereas current U.S. preferences are unilateral and at the mercy of congressional whims. Mercosur is also negotiating with Peru, indeed, with the Andean Community as a whole, with the objective of establishing an FTA between the two groupings. A joint declaration issued in August 2003 after a meeting in Lima between Presidents Lula of Brazil and Toledo projected that there would be a Mercosur–Andean

Community FTA by the end of this year. That document puts much stress on physical integration between the countries in the two regional groupings.

Peru last year had $7.6 billion of exports, about 25 percent to the United States. Peru's main exports are gold, copper, and fishmeal, but the idea of an FTA with either Mercosur or the United States (or both) is to diversify into other products for which tariff preferences would have more meaning.

One other story that made news in the financial press during this past month was the rejection by the United States Export-Import Bank of $214 million in loan guaranties for a natural gas project in a rain forest in the Amazon for shipment by pipeline over the Andes to Lima and a liquefied natural gas plant on the Peruvian coast. This is part of the Camisea project whose overall cost is expected to exceed $1.6 billion. The rejection was based on concern about the impact of the project on a sensitive, biologically diverse region. The board of the Inter-American Development Bank, on September 10, approved a $135 million loan for the Camisea project; the United States abstained on the vote.

Peru has had a difficult political history during recent decades and its democracy is still far from having matured. The electorate has a tendency to go off on tangents and choose leaders based less on solid information about them than on sentiments that can change almost overnight, as is taking place with Toledo. This is understandable in that a great part of the population is not part of the country's economy and their deepest interests have to be with the here and now, not with what might develop in the years to come. The social situation is complex and not amenable to rapid change toward more equality. Peru's leaders want to diversify the economy through diversification of production and exports, and bring the country into the regional and world economy. The latter is exemplified in the objective of separate FTAs with the United States and Mercosur, support of the FTAA, and improving the regional infrastructure as it affects Peru.

Note

[1] As a matter of interest, Chile, on September 11, remembered the thirtieth anniversary of the overthrow of the Allende government by the military forces under the leadership of Augusto Pinochet.

48 LATIN AMERICA AT YEAR-END 2003*

Latin America has had a spell of bad years in this new century. Real growth in gross domestic product was about 1.5 percent in 2003, according to a preliminary projection by the UN Economic Commission for Latin America and the Caribbean. In per capita terms, this translates into zero growth. The best one can say about this economic performance is that it was better than in either 2001 or 2002.

A GDP figure combining 20 countries (the Caribbean is not included in the foregoing calculation) has symbolic meaning, but does not speak to the situation in particular countries. Mexico had its third consecutive year of per capita GDP decline. Brazil did a little better; it had zero per capita GDP growth over these three years. Venezuela's overall GDP fell by about 13 percent. Argentina had 5.5 percent overall growth in 2003, but this followed four successive years of sharp decline. Interestingly, Colombia, despite its problem with terrorists and public safety, grew more than the other populous countries mentioned, but it did not do all that well.

The focus on GDP, overall and per capita, has meaning because it is the one economic indicator that defines the ability of countries to deal with their social needs. The official GDP figures should not be taken as gospel because they omit informal activities that make up about 50 percent of most Latin American economies. (I prefer this description to the phrase "underground economy" because the people involved work in plain sight.) Nevertheless, the official GDP can be compiled year after year with some consistency and is the basis for tax collections and, hence, social expenditures for education, health care, and security. The disappointing economic outcomes, coupled with low levels of tax collections in almost all Latin American countries, make it impossible to do much to alleviate the high level of poverty that permeates the region.

Politics are also fragile throughout Latin America. An elected Bolivian president was ousted in 2003 after street demonstrations, continuing a pattern that has become common in recent years. In the "old" days, that is, before the 1980s, the military frequently stepped in when it was dissatisfied with elected presidents. That is now frowned on—it

---

* *Issues in International Political Economy*, no. 48 (December 2003).

does not conform to the democracy charter agreed in the Organization of American States in September 2001—and the ousters are now managed by a more sophisticated technique. Street demonstrations and protests, sometimes abetted by the military, have led to the removal of elected heads of government in recent years in Peru, Argentina, and Ecuador, in addition to Bolivia. The succession after the ousters has tended to follow constitutionally mandated rules. The outward manifestations of democracy apparently still survive, but the end result is similar to the old system of *golpes* (overthrow of governments).

There is some good news to report in the hemisphere. Inflation, on which Latin America had the original patent, is now generally under control. The media are largely free and boisterous throughout the region. The trappings of democracy are now considered sacrosanct, and perhaps, one day, democracy itself may emerge full bloom. Corruption is omnipresent, but also universally condemned. Judicial systems are deficient in just about all countries, but this reality is now recognized. All of this is thin gruel compared with what should prevail in Latin America, but the relevant problems are now discussed in open public debate. Earlier, they were truly underground issues.

U.S. relations with Latin America are in equally bad shape. This may not be an apt comparison, but one would hope that the U.S. government could be part of the hemispheric solution. Instead, the United States—with some sporadic exceptions—is largely indifferent to its own hemisphere. This became evident after 9/11 because the immediate security threats were mostly elsewhere. The one policy instrument that the U.S. government was willing to wield was trade, in the form of a proposal for a Free Trade Area of the Americas (FTAA), but even here the enthusiasm seems to be waning. It might be more accurate to state that the U.S. posture is shifting away from a comprehensive FTAA in favor of bilateral free-trade agreements (FTAs) throughout the Americas. U.S. free trade with 14 hemispheric countries is either in place, under negotiation, or planned.

The FTAA process involves 34 countries, including the United States. Even if the United States concludes bilateral or plurilateral FTAs with all 33, this would be a far cry from a single FTAA. U.S. bilateral FTAs are hub-and-spoke agreements under which only the United States enjoys free trade with all the other signatories. They would add to the spaghetti of separate agreements that already exist in Latin America and thereby aggravate the complexity of disparate rules of origin and complex cross-discrimination. They would not—as the FTAA would—promote trade among the Latin American countries any more than now exists. The one positive policy instrument of U.S. policy toward the region would have been abandoned. Instead of pulling the hemisphere together, all these separate bilaterals would pull it further apart and impel the individual countries to look to Uncle Sam for export expansion.

At a recent meeting in Rio on trade, a Latin American delegate told me that although his country was pleased to be included as a prospective FTA partner with the United States, the unlikelihood of a thoroughgoing FTAA any time soon gave his country no other choice. His country, like many others in Latin America, would prefer a comprehensive FTAA.

Apart from trade, the United States has little going for it in the hemisphere. Latin American countries are used to U.S. unilateralism in making foreign policy, but the concern skyrocketed during the lead-up to the invasion of Iraq. Public opinion polls in just about every hemispheric country—other than Colombia, which has its own internal terrorist problems—show that up to 90 percent of respondents do not have a favorable view of the United States. It is not overstatement to say that the only point of real agreement among the countries of Latin America is their unease over the adventurous unilateralism of the United States. Is this reversible? Probably yes, to some extent, but only if the United States demonstrates a real interest in the fate of the countries of the hemisphere.

This is a pessimistic evaluation of the current situation in Latin America and of U.S. relations with the countries of the region. There are some points of hope. Brazil did not implode after Lula was elected, as many foreign analysts expected, but instead pulled together to avoid a debt workout after Lula showed that he could be a responsible leader. Mexico is not growing, but it is financially stable, which is more than could have been said during its financial crises of 1982 and 1994-95. Chile continues to perform well; some have put this reality into what used to be said about Israel—"A good country in a bad neighborhood." And the projections are for higher GDP growth in the region in 2004 than was the case in 2003. The upturn in the U.S. economy, by pulling in imports, should benefit Latin America. One can look at the silver linings as well as the ominous clouds—even as the ominous clouds remain in place.

This ambiguity has existed for a long time. Latin America, with its largely Western culture, has been unable to develop solid, durable democracies. Its growth patterns have been sporadic, replete with down as well as up periods. One can cite the lost decade of the '80s, the uptick in the first half of the '90s, and the current sluggishness and stagnation. Civic and official institutions are weak, including judicial systems that are not trusted either by foreign investors or by local populations. The region has a deserved reputation for considerable corruption. It has long been the worst region of the world with respect to income inequality. East Asian countries overtook those in Latin America in their development performance after World War II. It would take much more than a brief essay to understand the sociology that explains this less than stellar performance over such an extended period.

The most important concern of the population in practically all the large cities of the region—Sao Paulo and Rio, Buenos Aires, Bogotá, Mexico City, and others—is personal safety and security. This is a worldwide phenomenon, but the kidnappings, murders, robberies, and muggings are probably more pervasive in Latin America than elsewhere. An official of a large multinational corporation told me that when the regional representatives from the hemisphere meet in a Latin American city, the first order of business is for all of them to show that they have their instructions in their pockets or briefcases about what to do if they are kidnapped. Precise data on lawlessness are unknown due to the reluctance of citizens to inform the police when a crime against them is committed. Indeed, one bit of advice from old-timers to newcomers in most of these cities is to not report criminal acts against homes and persons to the police.

Yet, the seeds of political, economic, and social development are there. Leaders are well educated, an active middle class exists, and the region is full of enterprising business entrepreneurs. Resources devoted to primary and secondary education are inadequate and dropout rates are high, but the region is also blessed with first-rank universities. Much foreign investment finds its way to the region. It would be nice to be able to make an optimistic year-end report a year from now.

INDEX

Page numbers followed by the letters f and n refer to figures and notes, respectively.

Libya, 105, 106–107
Lula da Silva, Luis Inácio: economic policy
  issues, 54, 153, 154–155, 163, 203; FTAA
  prospects, 191; inter-American relations,
  196; Latin America herd tendency, 172;
  Peru trade objectives and, 199–200; reform
  agenda of, 128, 177–180, 192

Mahuad, Jamil, 58, 128, 151
Mao Zedong, 64, 85
Massachusetts, Burma boycotts, 98–100
Meltzer, Allan, 62, 72, 73
Menem, Carlos, 58, 128, 189, 191
Mercantilism, 5, 23
Mercosur: Argentina policy challenges, 190,
  191; Brazil-U.S. relations, 130, 132n; Chile-
  U.S. relations, 134, 135; dollarization
  debate, 58, 60; EU FTA possibility, 22;
  inter-American relations, 193, 194, 195–
  196; members of, 1, 132n; open market as
  option, 38; Peru trade objectives, 199–200;
  trade negotiation prospects, 51, 52; U.S.
  policy repeats self, 43
Mexico: Brazil comparisons, 129, 151; Cana-
  da-U.S. relations and, 182, 183; democracy
  issues, 70–71, 119–120, 123, 124, 146;
  dollarization debate, 57–58, 59, 60, 117;
  economic policy issues, 54, 55, 141, 142–
  144, 145–147, 163, 174–176; energy issues,
  127, 146, 173, 174, 175, 187; fertility rate in,
  96; financial rescue issues, 72–75; foreign
  relations and small actions, 88–89; FTAA
  prospects, 165, 167, 168, 191; GDP changes
  in, 145, 174–175, 176, 201; globalization
  issues, 64, 66; immigration issues, 92, 94,
  95, 101–103, 109, 110–111, 174, 187; inter-
  American relations, 127, 196; labor-trade
  link, 10, 11; Latin America-U.S. relations,
  126, 127, 128, 157, 158, 185, 187; multilateral institution roles, 62–63; NAFTA and
  energy, 173; NAFTA and export increases,
  13f; NAFTA evaluation, 13–16; NAFTA
  importance, 126, 127; nationalism issues,
  127, 173–176; open market as option, 38,
  39; policy priority issues, 85; presidential
  succession in, 189; sovereignty issues, 113,
  115, 116, 117; trade and development, 1, 2,
  3, 4; trucking services disallowed, 31–32,
  113, 116, 138; U.S.-Mexico relations, 56,
  127, 137–140, 148, 174, 185; U.S. policy

ambiguity, 46–47; U.S. policy repeats self,
  42, 43; year-end status, 70–71, 145–148,
  201, 203
Miami FTAA summit, 39, 52–53, 165
Middle East: democracy issues, 122, 124;
  foreign relations and small actions, 90;
  terrorism issues, 76, 78, 84, 85–86. See also
  specific countries
Moral hazard issues, 72–74
Morocco, 47
Most-favored-nation (MFN) principle:
  conditional vs. unconditional trade, 42–
  44; global economy year-end highlights,
  68; trade and development, 5–6; U.S.
  Congress and trade, 32; U.S. policy ambiguity, 45; U.S. policy repeats self, 41–44;
  WTO ruling on FSCs, 35
Multilateral institutions: demonstrations
  against as tool, 63, 69–70; role of, 17–20,
  56, 61–63, 115; trade issues facing Bush,
  21. See also Nongovernmental organizations; specific institutions
Multinational corporations: economic policy
  issues, 56; globalization issues, 64–66;
  Latin America security issues, 204; multilateral institution roles, 63; NAFTA evaluation, 13–14; trade negotiation prospects,
  51; trade policy after Seattle, 9; WTO
  ruling on FSCs, 68. See also Business
  interests
Myanmar. See Burma

Nader, Ralph, 12, 13–14, 61, 115
National Action Party, 70, 124
National Foreign Trade Council (NFTC), 98–
  99
National security issues: Canada-U.S. rela-
  tions, 181–182, 183; economic sanctions
  and, 105, 107; immigration policy and, 92,
  109, 111; Latin America-U.S. relations, 56;
  Latin America year-end status, 202, 204;
  sovereignty argument and, 114, 116, 117;
  U.S. economic stimulus and, 80. See also
  Terrorism
Nationalism: inter-American relations, 127,
  196; Mexico's, 127, 173–176; open market
  as option, 37; trade policy after Seattle, 9
Natsios v. National Foreign Trade Council, 98–99
Natural gas resources: Mexico, 127, 146, 173,
  175, 187; Peru, 200

ABOUT THE AUTHOR

Sidney Weintraub is director of the CSIS Americas Program and the senior scholar at CSIS who specializes in Western Hemisphere issues. In addition, he holds the William E. Simon Chair in Political Economy at CSIS. He is also professor emeritus at the Lyndon B. Johnson School of Public Affairs of the University of Texas at Austin.

A member of the U.S. Foreign Service from 1949 to 1975, Dr. Weintraub held the post of deputy assistant secretary of state for international finance and development from 1969 to 1974 and assistant administrator of the U.S. Agency for International Development in 1975. He has also been a senior fellow at the Brookings Institution. His most recent books are *Financial Decision-Making in Mexico: To Bet a Nation* (Pittsburgh, 2000) and *Development and Democracy in the Southern Cone: Imperatives for U.S. Policy in South America* (CSIS, 2000). He is coauthor of *The NAFTA Debate: Grappling with Unconventional Trade Issues* (Lynne Rienner, 1994) and author of *NAFTA at Three: A Progress Report* (Praeger/CSIS, 1997), *A Marriage of Convenience: Relations between Mexico and the United States* (Oxford, 1990), and *Free Trade between Mexico and the U.S.?* (Brookings, 1984). He received his Ph.D. in economics from the American University.